The Hormonal Compass

The Hormonal Compass

Matthew Petchinsky

1

The Hormonal Compass: Navigate Back to Your Youth

By: Matthew Petchinsky

Disclaimer

The Hormonal Compass: Navigate Back to Your Youth is a creative, educational, and informational wellness guide inspired by biohacking studies, alternative wellness practices, and longevity research. This book is **not** written by medical professionals, nor does it replace individualized medical care, diagnosis, or treatment.

The concepts, techniques, and protocols described throughout this guide draw from a mixture of publicly available research, anecdotal reports, age-reversal strategies, and holistic methodologies. While these approaches may support general well-being, hormonal balance, and improved vitality, they are **not universal**, and results can vary significantly from person to person based on genetics, medical history, existing diagnoses, medications, and lifestyle factors.

Because hormonal systems are complex and highly sensitive, any attempt to modify, optimize, or influence them—whether through supplements, biohacking practices, dietary changes, or lifestyle adjustments—should be done with **professional supervision**. Always consult a qualified **endocrinologist**, hormone specialist, or licensed medical provider before implementing any hormone-related strategies, including but not limited to:

- Supplements or herbals marketed for hormonal support
- Bioidentical hormone replacement therapies
- Peptide or longevity therapies
- Fasting or nutritional protocols that alter endocrine function
- Sleep, light, or circadian interventions aimed at hormone regulation
- Any protocol that claims to increase youthfulness, vitality, or longevity

The author and publisher make no guarantees regarding outcomes and disclaim any liability for injury, adverse reactions, or consequences resulting from the application of the information presented in this book. Readers are responsible for their own choices, health decisions, and the safe application of all wellness practices.

By continuing with this guide, you acknowledge that all information is offered for **educational purposes only**, and you agree to seek personalized medical guidance before making changes that may affect your hormonal health or overall well-being.

Introduction

Your hormones aren't working against you — they're just lost. Let's give them a map.

Hormones are not villains. They are messengers, translators, navigators, and negotiators running millions of microscopic conversations inside your body every single day. When those messages get scrambled, delayed, or distorted—through stress, aging, environment, diet, trauma, or simply life—your body doesn't betray you. It simply becomes **disoriented**. What feels like fatigue, weight gain, emotional turbulence, or accelerated aging is often the result of signals that have wandered off their original route.

The Hormonal Compass: Navigate Back to Your Youth exists to bring those signals home.

Modern biohacking reveals something extraordinary: your hormones are not fixed, rigid, or doomed to decline. They are **adaptable**, **trainable**, and—when guided properly—capable of returning to more youthful patterns of communication. Your body is not broken; it is responding to the map it has. When the map becomes outdated, you don't punish the traveler. You update the route.

This guide teaches you how to do exactly that.

Drawing from alternative wellness strategies, hormone-supportive habits, circadian balancing, stress-load reduction, targeted nutrients, and longevity-inspired practices, this book will help you understand and recalibrate the "big six" endocrine signals that shape how young or old you *feel*:

- **Cortisol** — your stress compass
- **Insulin** — your metabolic translator
- **Thyroid hormones** — your internal thermostat
- **DHEA** — your youth-preserving buffer
- **Estrogen & Testosterone** — your regenerative engines

When these signals are coordinated, your body doesn't just function—you thrive. Energy rises. Sleep deepens. Weight stabilizes. Skin brightens. Mood steadies. Focus sharpens. Biological age slows.

The synopsis you just read captures the essence:

From cortisol to DHEA, your hormones are the language of age. The Hormonal Compass teaches how to reset these signals and align your body with youthful balance.

This introduction is your first step toward understanding that age is not only chronological—it is **biochemical**, **behavioral**, and deeply **influenced by the conversations your hormones are having with each other**.

You are about to learn how to rewrite that conversation.

By the end of this book, you'll have a practical, clear, actionable map—a compass—to help your hormones find their way back to balance, vitality, and youthful coherence. Your body remembers how to be young. Your hormones simply need to be shown the way.

Chapter 1 – The Lost Signals

Understanding aging through testosterone, estrogen, cortisol, and melatonin decline

Aging is not merely a number—it's a shift in messaging. Your hormones speak in signals, rhythms, and biochemical pulses. When those signals weaken, distort, or fade, the body stops recognizing the instructions that once kept you vibrant, resilient, and hormonally coordinated. Testosterone, estrogen, cortisol, and melatonin are four of the most important regulators of youthfulness, and each one plays a critical role in shaping your energy, mood, metabolism, cellular repair, and how "young" your body feels. Understanding their decline is the first step toward navigating your way back to balance.

TESTOSTERONE: The Decay of Drive

Testosterone is more than a "male hormone"—it is the engine of vitality for all humans. In youth, testosterone pulses follow a steady, strong rhythm that fuels muscle growth, mental sharpness, assertiveness, metabolic stability, and deep cellular repair. As this hormone declines, the body loses one of its most powerful stabilizing forces. Its fall is gradual but profound, creating a cascade of subtle dysfunctions that accumulate quietly over time: slower recovery, decreased motivation, reduced strength, and the erosion of once-effortless confidence.

Biologically, testosterone decline begins earlier than most people expect—often in the late 20s, with a measurable drop each decade. Stress, poor sleep, high body fat, nutrient deficiencies, and chronic inflammation accelerate this decline, pushing the body into a metabolic pattern synonymous with aging. Testosterone controls the pace of protein synthesis, meaning that when the signal weakens, the body becomes less efficient at rebuilding what daily life breaks down. This is why aging begins not with big failures but with small recoveries that never happen.

One of the most misunderstood aspects of testosterone decline is its psychological impact. Low levels reduce dopamine sensitivity, altering drive, ambition, and emotional resilience. Tasks that once sparked excitement now feel draining. The "fire" of initiation—the urge to start something new, push harder, or take action—begins to fade. This is the hormonal signature of aging: not deterioration, but *diminished responsiveness.* Your hormones aren't fighting you—they're simply whispering in a world where they once roared.

Low testosterone also interacts heavily with metabolic health. It disrupts insulin sensitivity and encourages fat accumulation—especially visceral fat around the organs. This type of fat produces inflammatory signals that further sabotage testosterone production, creating a loop where aging accelerates itself. When this happens, even modest weight gain can spiral into hormonal stagnation, leaving the body feeling "sluggish," inflamed, and trapped in premature aging cycles.

Additionally, testosterone decline alters how well your body handles stress. In balanced levels, testosterone works as a stabilizing counterpart to cortisol, preventing stress from overwhelming the system. But when testosterone drops, cortisol faces no opposition, amplifying anxiety, irritability, and emotional volatility. The world feels heavier, and the nervous system becomes more sensitive to stimuli that were once easy to handle. This emotional shift is often mistaken for personality changes, when in reality, it is a biochemical signal crying out for recalibration.

The good news is that testosterone decline is neither final nor irreversible. Through targeted biohacking, nutrient support, optimized sleep cycles, and lifestyle interventions that restore hormonal rhythm, testosterone can often be revitalized to more youthful levels. The body remembers how to produce vitality—it simply needs a reason to start again. Understanding this hormonal descent is the first step in learning how to climb back out of it.

Testosterone is the pulse of vitality, the biochemical signature of initiative, strength, and biological momentum. In youth, this hormone flows in strong waves that instruct the body to repair tissue rapidly, burn fat efficiently, stabilize mood, and generate the deep internal confidence associated with health and momentum. When testosterone begins to decline, the body quietly loses one of its master signals of youthfulness. The earliest signs are often subtle—the loss of morning energy, reduced ambition, slower recovery from exertion, or a sense of diminished "spark." These are not personality changes; they are shifts in hormonal frequency.

Testosterone decline begins long before most people realize it. By the late twenties, the first measurable drop starts, progressing decade by decade. Modern life accelerates this decline dramatically through chronic stress, poor sleep, excessive environmental estrogen, nutrient deficiencies, and sedentary habits. As testosterone decreases, the body becomes less efficient at protein synthesis, weakening structural tissues like muscle, bone, and even the fascia that governs posture and movement. Aging does not begin with visible decline—it begins with microscopic repair gaps that accumulate quietly.

Psychologically, low testosterone alters how the brain interacts with reward systems. Dopamine becomes less effective, reducing motivation, focus, and the ability to experience deep satisfaction. Tasks once approached with enthusiasm now feel heavier, mentally demanding, or overwhelming. This hormonal shift can mimic depression or burnout, but the truth is simpler: the biological drive signal has weakened. This distinction is critical, because a lost signal can be restored, whereas a "broken personality" cannot.

Low testosterone profoundly impacts metabolism. It disrupts insulin sensitivity, promotes visceral fat storage, and slows metabolic rate. Fat stored around the organs is hormonally active, releasing inflammatory compounds that further suppress testosterone production. This creates a self-reinforcing cycle: hormonal decline drives inflammation, which drives further hormonal decline. The metabolism becomes sluggish, unresponsive, and resistant to change not because the body is stubborn, but because the hormonal instructions have changed.

Emotionally, testosterone decline destabilizes stress resilience. Testosterone normally counterbalances cortisol, smoothing emotional reactivity and strengthening confidence during adversity. When testosterone drops, cortisol becomes more dominant, increasing irritability, anxiety, and emotional sensitivity. Small stressors feel magnified, and the world becomes more overwhelming. Many interpret this shift as mental instability or emotional weakness. In reality, it is simply a missing biochemical buffer.

Fortunately, testosterone decline is one of the most reversible aspects of aging. Through sleep optimization, circadian repair, resistance training, nutrient support, stress regulation, and lifestyle interventions that increase androgen sensitivity, the body can often restore testosterone production to more youthful rhythms. Even without medication, the system can remember how to behave once the right internal environment is created. Decline is not destiny—it is a signal waiting to be redirected.

TESTOSTERONE NATURAL REMEDIES

Testosterone thrives when the body has access to minerals, healthy fats, and hormonal precursors that support steroidogenesis. Zinc, magnesium, and boron are three foundational minerals that directly raise testosterone by boosting luteinizing hormone, supporting testicular function, and increasing free testosterone by reducing SHBG. Foods such as oysters, pumpkin seeds, cacao, almonds, and avocados become essential nutritional tools because they deliver these minerals in highly absorbable forms. Incorporating nutrient-dense whole foods is one of the most efficient natural methods for building testosterone—especially in individuals depleted by stress or poor sleep.

Healthy fats are indispensable for testosterone production because your body synthesizes testosterone from cholesterol. Diets too low in fat often correlate with low testosterone, emotional instability, and decreased libido. Consuming olive oil, grass-fed butter, coconut oil, and fatty fish gives the body raw materials to restore androgen pathways. These fats stabilize cell membranes, nourish the nervous system, and improve androgen receptor sensitivity. When these fats become a staple rather than an afterthought, testosterone rises naturally without the crash-and-burn effect of stimulants or synthetic additives.

Adaptogenic herbs also play a major role in revitalizing testosterone. Ashwagandha reduces cortisol, which indirectly raises testosterone by eliminating hormonal competition. Tongkat Ali (Eurycoma longifolia) enhances androgen receptor sensitivity and increases free testosterone by reducing SHBG. Fenugreek supports metabolic balance and enhances libido. Shilajit, rich in fulvic acid, improves mitochondrial energy, thereby enhancing testosterone production at the cellular level. These herbs, taken consistently, rebuild androgen balance by reducing stress load and supporting hormone signal strength.

Nutritional timing is another overlooked natural method. Testosterone rises in the early morning, and the body prefers protein during the first meal to stabilize hormone production. When individuals begin their day with high-protein meals—such as eggs, grass-fed beef, Greek yogurt, or salmon—the endocrine system receives signals of strength, abundance, and metabolic stability. Conversely, high-sugar breakfasts spike insulin, suppress testosterone, and worsen fatigue. Eating in alignment with hormonal timing becomes a natural testosterone therapy.

Sunlight is also an extremely potent testosterone builder. UVB exposure increases Vitamin D, a hormone-like compound essential for testosterone synthesis. Just 15–20 minutes of sunlight on the skin each morning can raise testosterone levels, improve mood, stabilize circadian rhythm, and reduce depressive symptoms. Vitamin D deficiency is one of the most common causes of low testosterone, and sunlight serves as the most natural form of supplementation.

Finally, reducing xenoestrogen exposure is essential for restoring testosterone. Plastics, fragranced products, pesticides, and contaminated water deliver estrogen-mimicking chemicals that suppress androgen production and contribute to fat gain. Switching to glass containers, avoiding artificial scents, filtering water, and eating organic when possible dramatically reduces hormonal interference. Testosterone rises naturally when competing estrogenic chemicals are minimized.

TESTOSTERONE RECIPES

Recipe 1: The Androgen Rise Smoothie

A nutritional powerhouse designed to promote testosterone production, reduce inflammation, and fuel mitochondrial energy.

Ingredients:

- 1 cup Greek yogurt
- 1 tablespoon cacao powder
- 1 tablespoon pumpkin seeds
- 1 teaspoon maca root
- 1 teaspoon ashwagandha powder
- 1 tablespoon almond butter
- 1 cup blueberries
- 1 teaspoon honey
- 1 cup almond milk

Instructions:

Blend all ingredients until smooth. Drink in the early morning to align with the testosterone pulse window.

Recipe 2: Testosterone-Boosting Steak Bowl

Ingredients:

- 6 oz grass-fed steak
- 1 cup sautéed spinach
- 1 teaspoon garlic
- 1 tablespoon olive oil
- ½ avocado
- ¼ cup quinoa
- Sea salt & black pepper

Instructions:

Cook steak in olive oil with garlic until medium rare. Serve over quinoa with spinach and sliced avocado. This recipe provides zinc, iron, and healthy fats essential for testosterone regeneration.

Recipe 3: Mineral-Rich Power Broth

Ingredients:

- 4 cups bone broth
- 1 tablespoon sea salt
- 1 teaspoon turmeric
- 1 teaspoon black pepper
- 1 chopped onion
- 1 tablespoon coconut oil

Instructions:

Simmer all ingredients together for 15 minutes. Drink daily to replenish essential minerals that support hormonal balance.

(Space here)

Each of these recipes delivers minerals, fats, and amino acids that directly support testosterone production, repair tissues, and promote youthful vitality. When eaten consistently, they create an internal environment that allows androgens to rebuild steadily without stress.

TESTOSTERONE EXERCISES

Resistance training is the most powerful natural tool for raising testosterone. Compound movements such as squats, deadlifts, bench presses, and rows stimulate the entire endocrine system, triggering large surges of growth hormone and testosterone. These movements recruit multiple muscle groups simultaneously, creating metabolic stress that signals the body to enhance androgen output. Performing compound lifts 2–3 times weekly provides enough stimulus for long-term hormonal rebuilding without overtraining.

High-intensity interval training (HIIT) is another potent testosterone enhancer. Short bursts of intense effort followed by brief rest periods stimulate hormonal adaptation, fat burning, and metabolic optimization. A simple HIIT session might include sprinting for 20 seconds followed by 40 seconds of rest repeated for 10 rounds. This protocol increases testosterone sensitivity and improves insulin function, laying the foundation for hormonal restoration.

Slow, controlled strength training—especially with eccentric emphasis—builds muscle and increases androgen receptor density. This means testosterone becomes more effective, even if levels do not dramatically increase. Eccentric movements (slow lowering phases) generate microtears that encourage the body to produce more testosterone to heal and strengthen tissues. Consistency yields the greatest hormonal improvements.

Outdoor movement is another effective testosterone-boosting exercise. Hiking, walking in sunlight, and grounding barefoot on natural surfaces reduce cortisol, increase Vitamin D, and activate the parasympathetic nervous system. These shifts create optimal internal conditions for testosterone synthesis. The combination of movement and sunlight is uniquely restorative to the endocrine system.

Post-exercise recovery is equally important. Testosterone rises after training only if the body has adequate sleep, protein, and mineral intake. Without recovery, cortisol dominates and testosterone collapses. This is why training smarter—not harder—is essential for hormonal restoration. Building testosterone requires a balance between physical challenge and nervous system relaxation.

Finally, breathing exercises improve testosterone indirectly by reducing cortisol and improving oxygen flow to tissues. Practices like box breathing, diaphragmatic breathing, and Wim Hof–style methods stimulate hormonal pathways that support overall androgen production. Testosterone rises in bodies that feel safe, oxygenated, and energetically stable.

TESTOSTERONE ALTERNATIVE METHODS

Cold exposure is one of the most powerful alternative methods for increasing testosterone. Cold showers, ice baths, and cold-water immersion activate brown fat, reduce inflammation, and stimulate the luteinizing hormone responsible for testosterone production. The shock effect increases dopamine and improves androgen receptor sensitivity, creating a hormonal environment similar to youthful physiology.

Red light therapy is another potent modality. Red and near-infrared light stimulate mitochondrial function, improve cellular energy, and increase testosterone production in photoreactive tissues. Exposure to targeted wavelengths around 660 nm and 850 nm enhances blood flow, reduces inflammation, and promotes hormonal restoration. This method is widely used in longevity clinics but can be performed at home with proper devices.

Intermittent fasting improves testosterone by increasing human growth hormone, reducing insulin resistance, and stimulating autophagy. A fasting window of 14–18 hours allows the body to repair tissues, reduce inflammation, and increase sensitivity to hormonal signals. When combined with nutrient-dense meals, fasting can significantly enhance testosterone pathways.

Acupuncture supports testosterone by reducing cortisol, increasing blood circulation to endocrine organs, and stimulating meridians connected to reproductive health. This promotes hormonal equilibrium and supports long-term endocrine rejuvenation. Individuals with chronic stress often respond particularly well to acupuncture-based hormonal balancing.

Breathwork and meditation improve testosterone indirectly through nervous system regulation. When the parasympathetic nervous system is activated, luteinizing hormone increases, cortisol decreases, and androgen production becomes more efficient. Meditation also enhances dopamine pathways that support testosterone-driven behaviors like ambition, consistency, and focus.

Sexual activity also influences testosterone. Regular sexual engagement—without overstimulation—can increase testosterone levels significantly. Intimacy, touch, and sexual expression trigger hormonal cascades that improve mood, vitality, and endocrine responsiveness. This natural cycle is often disrupted by chronic stress, screen addiction, or emotional disconnect, but can be restored through intentional reconnection.

TESTOSTERONE-BOOSTING RECIPES (Ghee + Beef)

1. Ghee-Seared Steak with Garlic Sunlight Butter

Ingredients

- 8 oz grass-fed beef steak
- 1 tablespoon ghee
- 2 garlic cloves, crushed
- 1 teaspoon black pepper
- ½ teaspoon sea salt
- 1 teaspoon lemon juice
- Optional: fresh rosemary

Instructions

Heat ghee in a skillet until shimmering. Add steak and sear for 3–5 minutes each side. During the last minute of cooking, add crushed garlic and rosemary to the pan. Spoon the aromatic ghee over the steak until glossy and golden. Finish with sea salt, pepper, and a squeeze of lemon.

Benefits: Testosterone-supporting fats, zinc, iron, and creatine for recovery and androgen synthesis.

2. Testosterone Ghee Power Scramble

Ingredients

- 3 eggs
- 1 tablespoon ghee
- ½ cup spinach
- ¼ cup ground beef (cooked)
- 1 teaspoon turmeric
- Sea salt & pepper

Instructions

Heat ghee in a skillet, add spinach until wilted, then add ground beef. Whisk eggs with turmeric, salt, and pepper and pour into skillet. Cook to desired firmness.

Benefits: Eggs supply cholesterol (testosterone precursor), beef provides zinc, ghee stabilizes hormones.

Ginger Tea for Testosterone

Ginger increases testosterone production by stimulating the Leydig cells and improving blood flow to reproductive organs. Its anti-inflammatory properties reduce oxidative stress on testes and adrenal glands, creating an optimal environment for androgen synthesis. Studies show ginger raises luteinizing hormone, improves sperm quality, and boosts total testosterone—especially in stressed or inflamed bodies. Ginger tea taken daily supports mitochondrial function, which further enhances testosterone pathways.

ESTROGEN: The Erosion of Balance

Estrogen is the architect of internal harmony. Though often associated with reproduction, its influence extends far beyond fertility. Estrogen maintains bone density, stabilizes mood, protects the brain, regulates fat distribution, and supports youthful skin elasticity. When estrogen begins to decline, the body loses one of its most multifaceted protective signals. Aging accelerates not because the body "gets old," but because it loses the hormone responsible for orchestrating equilibrium.

The decline of estrogen affects individuals differently depending on sex, age, genetics, and metabolic health. In those assigned female at birth, estrogen drops sharply during perimenopause, creating rapid fluctuations that challenge memory, mood stability, and cardiovascular health. In those assigned male at birth, estrogen declines more gradually but no less meaningfully—impacting libido, joint lubrication, emotional processing, and bone strength. Despite cultural assumptions, everyone needs estrogen, and everyone suffers when its balance erodes.

One of estrogen's most underrated roles is its effect on the brain. Estrogen enhances synaptic plasticity, supports neurotransmitter regulation, and protects neural tissue from oxidative stress. When estrogen declines, brain fog becomes more common, memory weakens, and cognitive endurance shortens. This neurological dulling is not a sign of mental decline—it is a hormonal whisper that the brain's preferred fuel is running low.

Estrogen's decline also intensifies inflammation throughout the body. Estrogen helps regulate immune responses, keeping inflammatory markers under control. Without its moderating effect, the body tends to overreact, leading to joint discomfort, increased sensitivity to stress, and slower healing. Chronic low-grade inflammation then accelerates the aging process by damaging tissues more quickly than the body can repair them.

Additionally, declining estrogen disrupts metabolic pathways. It affects how the body stores fat, how well it processes glucose, and how efficiently it burns calories at rest. This shift can make weight management feel suddenly impossible, even when diet and habits remain unchanged. The metabolism is not failing; it is responding to a missing hormonal signal that once told it how to function.

Understanding estrogen decline is essential because it represents more than hormonal loss—it reflects the weakening of a system designed to harmonize the entire internal environment. When estrogen falls, the body loses balance. But balance can be restored. With proper strategies, nutrients, and lifestyle adjustments, the hormonal compass can be guided back toward equilibrium.

Estrogen is the hormone of internal harmony, coordination, and resilience. Although culturally framed as a reproductive hormone, estrogen is far more expansive. It modulates brain function, supports skin health, strengthens bones, regulates metabolism, lubricates joints, and maintains emotional equilibrium. When estrogen begins to decline, the body loses a central stabilizing force, and the aging process often accelerates drastically. This decline is not limited to women—everyone relies on estrogen for neurological and metabolic stability.

In individuals assigned female at birth, estrogen decline often begins in the mid-to-late 30s, intensifying during perimenopause. This creates fluctuations that affect mood, memory, sleep, and cardiovascular health. These changes are not random—they reflect the shifting rhythm of a hormone that once orchestrated hundreds of internal signals with ease. In individuals assigned male at birth, estrogen declines gradually, influenced heavily by body fat, liver function, and testosterone levels. Regardless of sex, low estrogen removes a key layer of internal protection.

One of estrogen's most profound roles is in the brain. It enhances synaptic connections, supports neurotransmitter regulation, protects neurons from oxidative stress, and improves learning and memory. When estrogen declines, brain fog becomes common, cognitive endurance weakens, and emotional resilience shifts. These changes often mimic early aging or mental fatigue, but they are simply the result of decreased estrogenic signaling in neural pathways.

Estrogen decline also impacts immune regulation. Estrogen helps the immune system respond appropriately—strong when necessary, calm when unnecessary. When estrogen levels fall, the body becomes more likely to overreact with inflammation. Joint discomfort increases, tissue repair slows, and low-grade inflammation becomes a chronic background noise. This inflammation fuels accelerated aging by constantly taxing the body's repair systems.

Metabolism is another major casualty of estrogen decline. Estrogen plays a crucial role in regulating glucose tolerance, fat distribution, and thyroid function. As its levels drop, the body becomes more prone to storing fat—particularly in the abdomen—and less efficient at processing carbohydrates. This metabolic slowdown is not caused by lifestyle failure, but by hormonal change. Weight gain becomes more predictive of estrogen decline than diet alone.

Understanding the many layers of estrogen's influence is essential, because its decline represents the erosion of a system designed to maintain balance. While estrogen cannot remain high forever, the environment can be optimized to reduce inflammatory damage, protect cognitive function, and support metabolic health. Rebalancing this hormone's pathways helps restore harmony even when levels naturally shift.

ESTROGEN NATURAL REMEDIES

Estrogen thrives when the body is nourished with phytoestrogen-rich foods, anti-inflammatory nutrients, and minerals that support hormone receptor sensitivity. Foods such as flaxseeds, sesame seeds, chickpeas, pomegranates, and berries naturally support estrogen pathways through lignans and plant estrogens that gently mimic the body's own hormonal signals. These foods do not replace estrogen but help stabilize its fluctuations by regulating receptor activity.

Healthy fats play an essential role in promoting estrogen production. Foods like olive oil, almonds, salmon, avocado, and chia seeds contain omega-3s and monounsaturated fats that support reproductive hormones, nourish the brain, and restore cellular membranes. These fats reduce inflammation and support hormone production at the ovarian and adrenal levels. Diets low in fat often correlate with low estrogen, dry skin, joint pain, and emotional instability.

B vitamins—especially B6, B9, and B12—are critical for estrogen metabolism and neurotransmitter support. Leafy greens, eggs, nutritional yeast, dark chocolate, and lentils provide these essential nutrients. When estrogen declines, mood instability becomes more pronounced because serotonin pathways weaken. B vitamins support these pathways and reduce estrogen-related emotional shifts.

Adaptogens like maca root, red clover, and black cohosh balance estrogen by supporting endocrine function and reducing hormonal volatility. These herbs provide gentle support for estrogen pathways without overstimulating them. Maca in particular nourishes the hypothalamus and pituitary glands, regulating hormonal output and reducing symptoms associated with estrogen decline.

Magnesium is essential for estrogen balance. It helps regulate neurotransmitters, supports sleep quality, reduces inflammation, and enhances estrogen receptor sensitivity. Magnesium-rich foods like spinach, cacao, pumpkin seeds, and bananas become indispensable for hormonal restoration. When magnesium is low, estrogen cannot function properly—even if levels are adequate.

Hydration and detoxification also play major roles in estrogen balance. The liver is responsible for processing estrogen metabolites, and when the liver is overloaded with toxins or inflammatory compounds, estrogen metabolism becomes dysfunctional. Drinking herbal teas, increasing water intake, and reducing alcohol consumption significantly improve estrogen detox pathways. A detoxified liver is essential for stable estrogen levels.

ESTROGEN RECIPES

Recipe 1: The Estrogen Harmony Bowl

Ingredients:

- ½ cup cooked quinoa
- ½ cup chickpeas
- 1 tablespoon flaxseed
- 1 tablespoon sesame seeds
- ¼ cup pomegranate seeds
- ½ avocado
- Olive oil + lemon dressing

Instructions:

Combine quinoa, chickpeas, seeds, avocado, and pomegranate. Drizzle with olive oil and lemon. This bowl simultaneously nourishes estrogen pathways, supports fiber-driven detox, and stabilizes hormonal fluctuations.

Recipe 2: Omega-3 Estrogen Soup

Ingredients:

- 1 can salmon
- 4 cups vegetable broth
- 1 cup kale
- 1 tablespoon garlic
- 1 tablespoon olive oil
- ½ cup carrots
- Sea salt & turmeric

Instructions:

Simmer broth with garlic and turmeric. Add salmon, kale, and carrots until tender. This soup supports anti-inflammatory estrogen pathways and nourishes brain hormones.

Recipe 3: Estrogen-Balancing Smoothie

Ingredients:

- ½ cup blueberries
- 1 tablespoon chia seeds
- 1 banana
- 1 teaspoon maca
- Almond milk
- 1 tablespoon almond butter

Blend until smooth. This smoothie provides phytonutrients, magnesium, and adaptogens essential for hormonal balance.

These recipes combine anti-inflammatory foods, phytoestrogens, and essential fats to create stability and resilience within estrogen pathways.

ESTROGEN EXERCISES

Strength training supports estrogen production by stimulating bone density and metabolic function. Exercises such as lunges, glute bridges, squats, and resistance band workouts improve estrogen receptor activity and enhance circulation to reproductive organs. Regular strength training reduces the risk of osteoporosis and stabilizes emotional health.

Low-impact cardio—such as brisk walking, swimming, or cycling—improves blood flow, reduces stress, and enhances the body's ability to regulate estrogen. Unlike high-intensity training, which can increase cortisol and disrupt hormones, low-impact cardio supports gentle hormonal balance. Performing these activities consistently strengthens metabolic rhythm.

Yoga is particularly beneficial for estrogen. Poses such as supported bridge, child's pose, and reclining bound-angle help regulate blood flow, reduce cortisol, and support uterine and ovarian health. Yoga also reduces inflammation and enhances nervous system stability, which protects estrogen pathways during hormonal transitions.

Pilates strengthens deep core muscles and promotes pelvic alignment, improving circulation to the endocrine organs located in the pelvic region. Better circulation improves nutrient delivery and supports hormonal stability.

Deep stretching and mobility work increase estrogen receptor sensitivity by improving fascia health. Estrogen receptors exist in fascia tissue, and when fascia is tight or dehydrated, hormones struggle to signal properly. Regular stretching supports hormonal communication.

Finally, mind-body movement—such as slow dancing, tai chi, or gentle flow workouts—reduces stress and promotes the emotional stability often disrupted by low estrogen. These movements stimulate serotonin and dopamine pathways, which rely on estrogenic regulation.

ESTROGEN ALTERNATIVE METHODS

Seed cycling is one of the most effective natural approaches to balancing estrogen. During the first half of the cycle, flax and pumpkin seeds support healthy estrogen levels. During the second half, sunflower and sesame seeds support progesterone balance. Even for individuals no longer cycling, seed rotation provides hormonal nourishment and stabilizes estrogenic pathways.

Acupuncture regulates estrogen by stimulating meridians connected to reproductive health. It reduces inflammation, balances liver detox pathways, and enhances blood flow to endocrine organs. Many individuals experience reduced hot flashes, improved mood, and more stable energy with regular acupuncture.

Herbal infusions, such as red clover tea or nettle leaf, support estrogen receptors and nourish the blood. These herbs contain phytoestrogens that gently mimic natural hormones. Drinking these infusions daily provides slow, steady hormonal restoration.

Aromatherapy with essential oils like clary sage, lavender, and geranium influences hormonal balance through the nervous system. These oils reduce cortisol, stabilize mood, and support estrogenic balance. Aromatherapy can be used through diffusers, baths, or direct inhalation.

Breathwork, particularly long exhalation techniques, reduces cortisol and supports estrogen. Because stress depletes estrogen, any method that reduces sympathetic activation helps restore hormonal balance. Breathwork restores emotional stability and reduces estrogen-related anxiety.

Castor oil packs placed on the abdomen support liver detox and improve estrogen metabolism. The liver plays a major role in processing estrogen metabolites, and castor oil increases blood flow to detox pathways. This method is ancient, safe, and effective.

Estrogen-Harmony Veggie Ghee Stir Fry with Beef Strips

Ingredients

- 1 cup broccoli
- 1 cup spinach
- ½ cup carrots
- 6 oz thin beef strips
- 1 tablespoon ghee
- 1 tablespoon sesame seeds
- 1 tablespoon flaxseed
- 1 tablespoon coconut aminos

Instructions

Heat ghee in pan. Cook beef strips until brown. Add veggies and stir fry until tender. Top with sesame seeds, flaxseed, and coconut aminos.

Benefits: Flax + sesame = phytoestrogens; beef maintains iron levels needed for estrogen pathways.

Ghee-Basted Beef & Berry Bowl

Ingredients

- 6 oz cooked beef chunks
- 1 tablespoon ghee
- ½ cup blueberries
- ¼ cup pomegranate seeds
- 1 cup mixed greens
- 1 teaspoon balsamic vinegar

Instructions

Warm beef in melted ghee. Place over greens, top with berries and pomegranate. Drizzle balsamic on top.

Benefits: Berries support estrogen detox, ghee reduces inflammation, beef stabilizes iron–estrogen balance.

Ginger Tea for Estrogen

Ginger reduces inflammation in pathways that metabolize estrogen. It assists the liver in breaking down estrogen metabolites, making estrogen balance smoother and reducing estrogen dominance symptoms. Ginger also improves blood flow to the abdomen, ovaries, and uterine region, enhancing hormone receptor sensitivity. For individuals with low estrogen, ginger helps stabilize emotional fluctuations by supporting serotonin and dopamine pathways connected to estrogen regulation.

CORTISOL: The Stress Compass Gone Blind

Cortisol is the hormone of survival, structure, and alertness. In youth, cortisol follows a predictable pattern: high in the morning to wake you up, low in the evening to help you rest. With age—and especially with chronic stress—this rhythm collapses. Cortisol becomes erratic: too high when it should be low, too low when you need it most. This dysregulation is one of the earliest signs of systemic aging and often the most overlooked.

High cortisol accelerates the breakdown of tissues, increases blood sugar, steals resources from sex hormones, and shuts down deep sleep cycles. Low cortisol leaves you fatigued, unfocused, and unable to tolerate even small stressors. The tragedy of modern aging is that many people experience both extremes—burnout followed by depletion—without ever realizing these swings reflect a hormonal compass that has lost its direction.

When cortisol loses its rhythm, the nervous system becomes trapped in survival mode. You may feel constantly "on edge," tired but wired, reactive, or emotionally overwhelmed. This isn't a personality flaw—it's the physiological consequence of a hormone that was never designed to stay switched on. Cortisol should behave like a wave. With age, stress, and poor recovery, the wave becomes a storm.

Cortisol dysregulation also disrupts memory formation and executive function. High cortisol damages hippocampal neurons, impairing your ability to recall names, events, or details. Low cortisol undermines focus and motivation. These cognitive changes are often interpreted as "getting older," when they are simply reflections of a stress signal firing out of sync.

Furthermore, cortisol imbalance interferes with every major hormone system. It suppresses thyroid conversion, reduces testosterone production, increases insulin resistance, inflames tissues, and distorts circadian cycles. Aging is not caused by cortisol—it is accelerated by cortisol mismanagement. When cortisol is steady, the body feels ten years younger. When it fluctuates wildly, every biological system feels ten years older.

Despite its destructive reputation, cortisol is not the enemy. It becomes harmful only when misaligned. With targeted practices—such as sleep restoration, nervous system regulation, glucose management, and strategic stress unloading—the cortisol compass can be reset. When cortisol returns to rhythm, vitality follows.

Cortisol is both the anchor and the alarm system of the body. In youth, it follows a powerful circadian rhythm: rising sharply in the morning, falling gradually throughout the day, and reaching a minimum at night. This wave governs energy, alertness, emotional stability, and the ability to handle stress. As aging progresses—or when chronic stress dominates—this rhythm becomes distorted. Cortisol rises at the wrong times, falls when it should rise, or remains elevated constantly. This is the signature hormonal shift that makes aging feel "heavy."

High cortisol accelerates tissue breakdown, elevates blood sugar, suppresses thyroid function, and reduces the production of reproductive hormones. It drains the body of its ability to recover and adapt. When cortisol stays high for too long, it begins to damage the hippocampus, the brain region responsible for memory and emotional regulation. This leads to difficulty focusing, recalling information, or emotionally processing experiences. People often misinterpret this as cognitive decline, but it is hormonal misalignment.

Low cortisol is equally problematic. After years of chronic stress, the adrenal system becomes depleted, producing too little cortisol to maintain normal function. This creates severe fatigue, low mood, irritability, and an inability to respond to stress. Small tasks feel overwhelming; basic responsibilities feel monumental. This is not laziness or weakness—it is biochemical exhaustion caused by signal depletion.

The nervous system becomes trapped in survival mode when cortisol loses its rhythm. The body shifts into hypervigilance, unable to fully relax or feel safe. Nighttime becomes restless, mornings become sluggish, and the sensation of being "tired but wired" becomes common. This pattern is so normalized in modern society that many accept it as part of aging, but it is entirely reversible when the cortisol pattern is restored.

Cortisol imbalance disrupts every major hormone system. It reduces testosterone, interferes with estrogen balance, increases insulin resistance, disrupts thyroid conversion, and suppresses melatonin. The entire hormonal system becomes disorganized because cortisol is intended to function as the master regulator of energy and timing. When the regulator becomes unstable, all downstream hormones lose coherence.

Resetting cortisol requires systematic lifestyle alignment: improving sleep quality, stabilizing blood sugar, reducing inflammatory load, regulating nervous system responses, and restoring circadian rhythm. Once cortisol realigns, energy returns, emotional balance strengthens, and many signs of aging begin to reverse. Cortisol is not the enemy—it is a compass desperately trying to point north again.

CORTISOL NATURAL REMEDIES

Cortisol thrives when the body experiences predictable rhythms of safety, rest, nourishment, and support. Natural remedies for cortisol focus on reducing stress load, restore circadian rhythm, and lowering inflammation. Adaptogens like ashwagandha, rhodiola, tulsi, and reishi mushroom regulate the stress response by balancing the HPA axis. These herbs help the adrenal glands respond appropriately to stress instead of overreacting.

Magnesium is one of the most important minerals for cortisol regulation. It supports muscle relaxation, reduces anxiety, improves sleep, and calms the nervous system. Magnesium-rich foods like dark chocolate, leafy greens, pumpkin seeds, and bananas help the body relax. Supplemental magnesium glycinate or magnesium malate can further support relaxation.

Omega-3 fatty acids reduce cortisol by lowering inflammation and stabilizing mood. Foods like salmon, sardines, walnuts, and chia seeds support brain health and reduce overactive stress responses. These fats stabilize adrenal output and improve the body's ability to handle daily stress.

Vitamin C lowers cortisol by supporting adrenal function. Foods like oranges, strawberries, bell peppers, and camu camu powder help reduce cortisol levels and restore immune function. The body uses large amounts of Vitamin C during stress, making supplementation highly effective for cortisol regulation.

Herbal teas such as chamomile, lemon balm, and passionflower reduce cortisol by relaxing the nervous system. Drinking these teas before bedtime helps lower nighttime cortisol, allowing melatonin to rise naturally. These herbs support mental clarity and emotional regulation.

Grounding, earthing, and spending time in nature all support cortisol regulation. Walking barefoot on natural surfaces reduces inflammation, stabilizes brainwaves, and lowers cortisol quickly. Nature contact resets the nervous system and restores hormonal balance.

CORTISOL RECIPES

Recipe 1: Anti-Cortisol Stress Tea

Ingredients:

- 1 teaspoon chamomile
- 1 teaspoon lemon balm
- 1 teaspoon lavender
- 1 cup hot water
- 1 teaspoon honey

Steep herbs for 7–10 minutes. Drink before bed to lower nighttime cortisol and improve sleep.

Recipe 2: Cortisol-Calming Smoothie

Ingredients:

- Spinach
- Banana
- Chia seeds
- 1 teaspoon ashwagandha
- 1 teaspoon cacao
- Coconut milk

Blend until creamy. This smoothie supports adrenal health, reduces inflammation, and nourishes the nervous system.

Recipe 3: Omega-3 Stress Relief Bowl

Ingredients:

- 1 can salmon
- 1 tablespoon olive oil
- ½ cup brown rice
- ½ avocado
- Lemon juice
- Sea salt

This bowl stabilizes blood sugar, reduces inflammation, and supports cortisol regulation.

Ground Beef Ghee Nourish Bowl (Anti-Stress)

Ingredients

- 1 tablespoon ghee
- ½ lb ground beef
- ½ cup cooked rice
- ½ avocado
- 1 teaspoon turmeric
- 1 teaspoon cumin
- 1 teaspoon lemon juice

Instructions

Cook ground beef in ghee with turmeric and cumin. Serve over rice, top with avocado and lemon.

Benefits: Ghee + beef fat calm the nervous system; turmeric lowers inflammation linked to high cortisol.

Cortisol-Calming Beef Bone Broth with Ghee

Ingredients

- 3 cups beef bone broth
- 1 teaspoon ghee
- ¼ cup chopped spinach
- ¼ teaspoon sea salt
- Pinch black pepper

Instructions

Warm broth, stir in ghee until melted. Add spinach and simmer 5 minutes.

Benefits: Bone broth stabilizes blood sugar & adrenals; ghee nourishes the gut–brain axis.

CORTISOL EXERCISES

Walking is the single most effective cortisol-lowering exercise. Just 20–30 minutes of gentle walking reduces stress hormones, stabilizes mood, and improves metabolic health. Walking outdoors amplifies the benefits due to sunlight and nature exposure.

Yoga reduces cortisol through slow, controlled movements that stimulate the parasympathetic nervous system. Poses like child's pose, forward fold, and legs-up-the-wall regulate cortisol and promote relaxation. Yoga also improves sleep quality and emotional balance.

Pilates supports cortisol reduction by strengthening the core and improving posture. Better posture reduces physical stress on muscles and joints, which lowers cortisol. Pilates stabilizes the nervous system and enhances breath regulation.

Tai chi is a powerful cortisol-lowering exercise that improves balance, coordination, and nervous system regulation. Its slow, fluid movements increase parasympathetic activation and alpha brainwave activity, leading to calmness and improved endocrine stability.

Breathwork exercises—such as 4-7-8 breathing, box breathing, or slow diaphragmatic breathing—lower cortisol rapidly. Breathwork shifts the body from sympathetic dominance into relaxation mode, supporting cortisol balance and emotional stability.

Finally, restorative stretching supports cortisol reduction by releasing tight fascia. Tight fascia increases cortisol and restricts blood flow. Stretching improves circulation and reduces stress hormones.

CORTISOL ALTERNATIVE METHODS

Cold therapy used strategically can lower cortisol by training the nervous system to adapt to controlled stress. Short cold showers or brief cold immersion reduce inflammation and stabilize cortisol production. The key is exposure—not duration.

Sound healing methods like binaural beats, singing bowls, or low-frequency music lower cortisol by altering brainwave states. These methods activate theta and alpha wave patterns that promote relaxation.

Aromatherapy with lavender, bergamot, and sandalwood reduces cortisol by calming the limbic system. These oils can be used in diffusers, baths, or applied with carrier oils to promote deep relaxation.

Acupuncture supports cortisol regulation by affecting the HPA axis and improving the flow of energy through meridians associated with stress. Regular acupuncture sessions decrease cortisol spikes and improve hormonal balance.

EMDR tapping and acupressure reduce cortisol by resetting emotional pathways in the brain. These techniques are powerful for individuals who carry chronic emotional stress or trauma.

Meditation remains one of the most effective cortisol-lowering techniques. Regular meditation reduces cortisol, improves emotional regulation, and increases resilience. Even 10 minutes daily creates long-lasting hormonal benefits.

Ginger Tea for Cortisol

Ginger is an HPA-axis stabilizer. It reduces inflammation in the adrenal glands, improves insulin sensitivity, and lowers the cortisol spikes caused by stress or blood sugar crashes. Ginger tea induces parasympathetic relaxation, improving heart rate variability, reducing anxiety, and promoting a sense of grounded calm. This makes ginger one of the most reliable teas for lowering cortisol without sedation.

MELATONIN: The Vanishing Night Signal

Melatonin is far more than a sleep hormone. It is the body's primary regulator of circadian rhythm, mitochondrial repair, nighttime detoxification, and deep cellular rejuvenation. In youth, melatonin surges nightly, bathing tissues in signals that restore the nervous system, renew hormones, and repair oxidative damage. As melatonin declines with age—especially after the mid-30s—the body loses its most important "reset button."

Melatonin decline often begins without dramatic symptoms. Sleep becomes slightly lighter, slightly shorter, or slightly more fragmented. But these small disruptions compound into larger problems: poorer memory consolidation, reduced testosterone production, increased cortisol in the evening, and impaired metabolic regulation. Sleep quality alone can determine how "old" your body feels, and melatonin is the gatekeeper of sleep depth.

The modern environment accelerates melatonin loss dramatically. Blue light exposure, screens at night, elevated stress, artificial lighting, and erratic sleep patterns suppress melatonin more aggressively than aging itself. Many people experience melatonin patterns similar to someone 20 years older simply because their circadian environment is chronically disrupted.

Low melatonin also reduces the body's antioxidant capacity. Melatonin is one of the most potent antioxidants the body produces naturally. It protects mitochondria, repairs DNA, and neutralizes free radicals. When melatonin levels decline, the body becomes more vulnerable to oxidative stress, one of the core drivers of accelerated aging. Fatigue, inflammation, and cellular damage become more prominent when the night signal weakens.

Another overlooked effect of melatonin decline is hormonal imbalance. Melatonin regulates the timing of cortisol, growth hormone, thyroid function, insulin sensitivity, and even reproductive hormones. When melatonin weakens, hormone signaling becomes "noisy," delayed, or incomplete. This desynchronization disrupts everything from appetite to emotional regulation. Aging is not just a decline of hormones—it is the decline of the *choreography* that coordinates them.

Melatonin can be restored—not only through supplementation, but through behaviors that realign circadian rhythm. Dark-light cycles, temperature regulation, meal timing, stress reduction, and sleep rituals can all revive melatonin production. As melatonin rises, the body remembers how to repair itself at night, and the feeling of youthful recovery returns.

Melatonin is the body's nighttime architect, the conductor of deep restorative sleep, cellular rejuvenation, and circadian rhythm. It surges in darkness, instructing the brain to repair neurons, detoxify waste products, recalibrate hormones, and restore mitochondrial energy. As melatonin declines with age, these processes weaken. Sleep becomes lighter, less restorative, and more fragmented. The feeling of waking up tired becomes a silent signal of hormonal aging.

Melatonin levels drop naturally after the mid-30s, but modern life accelerates the decline significantly. Blue light exposure, artificial lighting, late-night screens, elevated nighttime cortisol, and irregular sleep schedules suppress melatonin even more powerfully than biological aging. Many people today have melatonin patterns that resemble those of someone 20 years older, simply because their circadian environment is disrupted.

When melatonin levels fall, the brain loses one of its strongest antioxidants. Melatonin protects DNA, reduces oxidative stress, and supports mitochondrial function. Without adequate melatonin, the brain becomes more vulnerable to inflammation and accumulates toxins more easily during the night. This leads to morning grogginess, slower thinking, emotional instability, and chronic fatigue that builds year after year.

Low melatonin also destabilizes hormonal timing. Cortisol rises earlier than it should. Testosterone production drops. Growth hormone release weakens. Insulin sensitivity declines. Thyroid signals become mistimed. Melatonin's decline creates a domino effect: when the night signal weakens, every daytime hormone shifts out of rhythm. The body begins living in a permanent state of circadian confusion.

Melatonin decline also impacts metabolic health. Deep sleep is when the body resets blood sugar levels, repairs pancreas function, and improves insulin sensitivity. Without strong melatonin, fewer metabolic repairs occur. This fuels stubborn fat gain, cravings, and impaired glucose tolerance. Many people try dieting, fasting, and exercise before realizing their metabolism is failing because their nighttime repair cycle has collapsed.

Fortunately, melatonin can be restored without relying solely on supplements. Dark-light cycles, temperature-based sleep cues, early morning sunlight exposure, evening light restrictions, stress reduction, and consistent sleep timing can dramatically increase natural melatonin production. Once melatonin is restored, energy, mood, weight regulation, and cellular repair all improve. The body remembers how to rejuvenate—it simply needs darkness and timing to activate those pathways.

MELATONIN NATURAL REMEDIES

Melatonin restoration begins with circadian rhythm repair. The body produces melatonin in darkness, so reducing nighttime light exposure is essential. Dimming lights after sunset, reducing screen time, and using warm lighting help melatonin rise naturally. Blue light suppresses melatonin for hours, making nighttime screens a major contributor to poor sleep and accelerated aging.

Magnesium supports melatonin production by relaxing muscles, calming the nervous system, and stabilizing GABA pathways. Magnesium-rich foods and supplements create an internal environment conducive to sleep. Without magnesium, melatonin cannot rise properly—even if sleep timing is ideal.

Herbs like valerian root, passionflower, lemon balm, and skullcap support melatonin production by calming the nervous system. Drinking herbal teas before bed helps initiate the sleep cycle. These herbs reduce nighttime cortisol spikes that suppress melatonin.

Tryptophan-rich foods—such as turkey, eggs, cheese, and nuts—support serotonin production. Serotonin converts to melatonin in the pineal gland. Eating tryptophan foods in the evening increases natural melatonin release.

Vitamin B6 supports melatonin synthesis by helping convert tryptophan into serotonin and melatonin. B6-rich foods include bananas, chickpeas, salmon, and dark leafy greens. Without B6, melatonin production becomes inefficient.

Ashwagandha and reishi mushrooms support nighttime melatonin by lowering stress hormones that interfere with sleep. These adaptogens stabilize the HPA axis and reduce nighttime cortisol, allowing melatonin to rise naturally.

MELATONIN RECIPES

Recipe 1: Sleep-Inducing Moon Milk

Ingredients:

- 1 cup warm almond milk
- 1 teaspoon ashwagandha
- ½ teaspoon cinnamon
- 1 teaspoon honey
- Pinch of nutmeg

Warm the milk, stir in ingredients, and drink before bed. This promotes relaxation and melatonin release.

Recipe 2: Serotonin-to-Melatonin Evening Bowl

Ingredients:

- ½ cup oats
- 1 banana
- 1 tablespoon peanut butter
- 1 teaspoon chia seeds
- Cinnamon

This bowl delivers tryptophan, magnesium, and complex carbs for natural melatonin production.

Recipe 3: Herbal Sleep Tea

Ingredients:

- 1 teaspoon valerian
- 1 teaspoon lemon balm
- 1 teaspoon passionflower
- 1 cup hot water

Steep and drink 30–60 minutes before bed.

Ghee-Infused Evening Beef & Sweet Potato Bowl

Ingredients

- 6 oz cooked beef
- 1 tablespoon ghee
- 1 cup mashed sweet potato
- ½ teaspoon cinnamon
- 1 pinch sea salt
- Optional: chamomile on the side

Instructions

Warm beef in a tablespoon of ghee. Serve over mashed sweet potatoes mixed with cinnamon and sea salt.

Benefits: Sweet potatoes support serotonin → melatonin pathway; ghee calms nighttime cortisol.

Serotonin–Melatonin Beef & Ghee Rice Soup

Ingredients

- 4 cups beef broth
- 1 tablespoon ghee
- ½ cup rice
- 1 small carrot
- 1 celery stalk
- Sea salt
- ¼ teaspoon turmeric

Instructions

Simmer broth with rice, carrot, celery until soft. Stir in ghee before serving.

Benefits: Warm carbs in the evening boost tryptophan entry into the brain → melatonin production enhanced.

MELATONIN EXERCISES

Evening stretching regulates melatonin by activating the parasympathetic nervous system. Gentle stretches for the hips, neck, shoulders, and lower back prepare the body for sleep.

Yoga Nidra is one of the most effective melatonin-boosting exercises. It slows brainwaves, relaxes the nervous system, and signals the pineal gland to release melatonin. Practicing Yoga Nidra before bed improves sleep quality dramatically.

Slow walking 1–2 hours before bed lowers cortisol and primes melatonin release. Evening walks reduce stress hormones and support deep sleep.

Breathwork, particularly slow nasal breathing, increases melatonin by relaxing the autonomic nervous system and lowering nighttime stress. Breathwork routines before bed dramatically improve sleep quality.

Gentle tai chi movements performed in the evening help synchronize the circadian rhythm and reduce nighttime cortisol. Tai chi trains the mind and body into a state of flow before sleep.

Foam rolling releases tension in the muscles and fascia, allowing the nervous system to relax. When the body is tense, melatonin cannot rise properly. Foam rolling supports nighttime hormonal alignment.

MELATONIN ALTERNATIVE METHODS

Red light therapy in the evening stimulates melatonin production by signaling to the circadian system that nighttime has arrived. Red wavelengths do not suppress melatonin like blue light does. Using red light in the evening promotes deep sleep.

Sound therapy with white noise or calming frequencies increases melatonin by relaxing the nervous system. These frequencies stabilize brainwaves and reduce nighttime anxiety.

Acupuncture supports melatonin by stimulating meridians associated with sleep, calming the nervous system, and reducing nighttime cortisol. Many experience deeper sleep after acupuncture sessions.

Weighted blankets support melatonin production by activating deep pressure receptors in the body, which calm the nervous system and trigger relaxation hormones.

Grounding—placing feet on earth in the early evening—resets circadian rhythms and stabilizes cortisol. When cortisol stabilizes, melatonin rises more effectively.

Meditation before bed enhances melatonin by reducing mental noise, calming the nervous system, and shifting brainwaves into alpha and theta states. These states support natural melatonin rise and deeper sleep.

Ginger Tea for Melatonin

By lowering evening cortisol, ginger indirectly increases melatonin production. Ginger also improves digestion, reducing nighttime stress on the gut—one of the major disruptors of melatonin. When mixed with warm liquids, ginger increases body temperature slightly, promoting a natural temperature drop afterward (which triggers melatonin). Ginger tea in the evening deepens sleep and enhances the serotonin → melatonin conversion cycle.

Universal Hormone-Rebuilding Ginger Tea

Perfect for all four hormone systems.

Ingredients:

- 1–2 inches fresh ginger root (sliced or grated)
- 2 cups water
- 1 teaspoon honey (optional)
- ½ teaspoon lemon (optional for morning, avoid at night)

Instructions:

Simmer the ginger in water for 10–15 minutes.

Strain, add honey if desired, and drink warm.

Morning = energizing

Evening = calming and cortisol-lowering

◈ Hormone-Specific Ginger Tea Variations

Testosterone Variation

Add:

- ½ teaspoon turmeric
- Pinch of black pepper
- 1 teaspoon ghee (optional)

This variation reduces inflammation and adds androgen-supportive fats and spices.

Estrogen Variation

Add:

- 1 teaspoon ground flaxseed
- 1 teaspoon sesame seeds (soaked overnight)
- A few pomegranate seeds

This supports phytoestrogen pathways and estrogen detox.

Cortisol Variation

Add:

- 1 teaspoon lemon balm
- ½ teaspoon chamomile
- Small pinch cinnamon

Perfect for deep relaxation and adrenal nourishment.

Melatonin Variation

Add:

- ¼ teaspoon nutmeg
- ¼ teaspoon lavender
- ½ teaspoon honey

Avoid lemon at night.

This version lowers nighttime cortisol and activates sleep signals.

GINGER TEA: THE UNIVERSAL HORMONAL RESTORATION ELIXIR

Ginger tea is one of the rare natural remedies that supports every major hormone discussed in this chapter: testosterone, estrogen, cortisol, and melatonin. Ginger works at the level of the mitochondria, the liver, the nervous system, and the endocrine glands—making it one of the most powerful, accessible, and globally recognized hormone-alignment tonics. Whether made with fresh ginger root or convenient store-bought tea bags, the compounds within ginger (gingerols, shogaols, zingerone) activate deep healing pathways that modern science continues to uncover. It is one of the simplest daily rituals a person can adopt, yet its impact is profound.

For testosterone, ginger increases luteinizing hormone, improves blood flow, and reduces inflammation in the testes and adrenal glands. Testosterone drops quickly when oxidative stress is high, and ginger directly lowers the oxidative load that suppresses androgen production. Regular ginger tea intake has been linked to higher free testosterone, improved libido, greater energy, and enhanced recovery from both stress and physical activity. Whether brewed from fresh ginger or taken from store-bought tea bags, the endocrine-supporting compounds remain active and effective.

For estrogen, ginger regulates inflammatory pathways that affect estrogen metabolism. Estrogen depends heavily on the liver's detoxification abilities, and ginger enhances phase I and phase II liver function. This reduces estrogen dominance symptoms, supports stable estrogen levels, and improves the sensitivity of estrogen receptors. Ginger tea also improves blood flow to the abdominal and pelvic regions, allowing reproductive organs to receive nutrients and oxygen more efficiently. This is especially important for individuals who experience mood shifts, low energy, or mental fog due to estrogen fluctuations.

For cortisol, ginger is one of nature's best HPA-axis soothers. It stabilizes blood sugar, reduces inflammation in adrenal tissues, and promotes a calm parasympathetic state. Drinking warm ginger tea—whether fresh or store-bought—can rapidly reduce cortisol spikes caused by stress, lack of sleep, or emotional overload. It is a natural anxiolytic that grounds the nervous system without sedation. For people dealing with chronic tension, chronic stress, or burnout, ginger tea becomes a daily anchor that retrains the body away from survival mode.

For melatonin, ginger helps establish a deeper, more restorative sleep cycle by lowering nighttime cortisol and improving digestive calm before bed. The gut and brain communicate constantly, and when digestion is strained, melatonin cannot rise properly. Ginger relaxes the digestive tract, reduces nighttime discomfort, and releases warmth through the body—followed by a natural cooling effect that signals the pineal gland to release melatonin. Drinking ginger tea in the evening (especially versions with lavender, nutmeg, or chamomile) creates an internal environment where melatonin can rise fully and consistently.

One of ginger tea's greatest strengths is its accessibility. Fresh ginger root provides the strongest therapeutic benefits, but **store-bought ginger tea bags** offer a fast, convenient alternative that still delivers hormone-supportive benefits. Individuals who cannot slice, boil, or simmer fresh ginger can simply steep a tea bag and receive much of the same endocrine nourishment. This makes ginger tea an inclusive remedy—anyone, regardless of schedule or cooking skill, can incorporate it into their hormonal restoration plan.

When used consistently—morning for testosterone and cortisol support, evening for estrogen stability and melatonin release—ginger tea becomes a daily hormonal alignment ritual. It harmonizes inflammation, stabilizes mood, strengthens metabolic pathways, and promotes youthful hormonal rhythm. Simple. Powerful. Universal. This tea becomes a compass-alignment tool, a warm signal to the body that healing is not only possible but already underway.

THE CHAIN REACTION EFFECT: WHEN ONE HORMONE FALLS, OTHERS FOLLOW

Hormonal aging does not occur in isolation. When one hormone declines, it influences the trajectory of several others. This creates cluster patterns—domino chains where one disrupted signal destabilizes an entire system. The most common chain reaction begins with cortisol dysregulation. Chronic stress raises cortisol, which suppresses testosterone, blunts estrogen receptors, impairs thyroid conversion, and disrupts melatonin. This creates a cascade of aging signals that accelerate one another.

As testosterone falls, insulin resistance increases, encouraging greater fat storage. Visceral fat releases inflammatory compounds that further suppress testosterone. This creates a feedback loop that worsens metabolic health, shrinks muscle mass, and lowers energy. The body becomes stuck in a pattern where hormonal decline accelerates the conditions that cause even more hormonal decline.

Estrogen decline interacts with these patterns as well. Lower estrogen reduces glucose tolerance, encourages inflammation, and destabilizes serotonin and dopamine pathways. When estrogen drops, cortisol becomes more reactive. This makes the nervous system more sensitive to stress, worsening melatonin suppression and further accelerating hormonal imbalance. Aging becomes a cycle, not a single event.

Melatonin loss interacts with testosterone decline by reducing nighttime growth hormone pulses. This leads to slower muscle repair, weaker immune function, and reduced mitochondrial regeneration. In turn, weak mitochondria increase fatigue and lower energy output, creating less physical activity and worsening hormonal decline. Metabolic slowdown follows naturally.

Thyroid hormones also become entangled in this chain. High cortisol suppresses active T3 production, slowing metabolism. Low testosterone reduces thyroid receptor sensitivity. Low estrogen weakens the thyroid's ability to regulate body temperature and energy. When thyroid function slows, the entire hormonal system becomes less responsive, reinforcing the cycle of aging.

Understanding the chain reaction effect empowers you to break it. You do not need to fix every hormone individually. By restoring circadian rhythm, lowering inflammation, stabilizing cortisol, and supporting core metabolic pathways, the entire hormonal network can begin recalibrating itself. Aging is not linear—it is feedback-driven. And feedback loops can be reversed.

THE MITOCHONDRIAL CONNECTION: WHERE AGING ACTUALLY BEGINS

At the heart of hormonal aging lies mitochondrial health. Mitochondria produce the energy that powers every cell, and hormones depend on mitochondrial signals to function properly. When mitochondrial energy declines, hormonal production, responsiveness, and timing decline with it. This is why aging often begins with fatigue—the mitochondria lose efficiency before hormones fully collapse.

Testosterone and estrogen both protect mitochondria by reducing oxidative stress, enhancing ATP production, and stabilizing metabolic pathways. When these hormones decline, mitochondrial membranes become more vulnerable to damage. This leads to slower energy production, increased fatigue, and reduced ability to recover from stress or exercise. What feels like low motivation is often mitochondrial insufficiency amplified by hormonal decline.

Cortisol has a complicated relationship with mitochondria. Short-term cortisol supports energy mobilization, but chronic cortisol elevation damages mitochondrial DNA, weakens the electron transport chain, and increases oxidative stress. This accelerates aging at the cellular level, leading to chronic tiredness, weight gain, and reduced cognitive function. When cortisol remains high, mitochondria suffer relentlessly.

Melatonin is one of the most powerful mitochondrial antioxidants the body produces. It directly enters mitochondria and neutralizes free radicals. As melatonin declines, mitochondrial damage accumulates more quickly. This loss of nighttime repair accelerates biological aging, making every system more vulnerable. The connection between melatonin and mitochondrial aging is one of the most important yet most overlooked aspects of longevity.

Mitochondrial decline creates hormonal resistance. Receptors become less responsive. Signals become weaker. The body requires more hormonal output to achieve the same effect. This is why people often feel older before their hormones test low. The hormones are present—but the cells cannot "hear" them because the energy system that powers receptor function is impaired.

Restoring mitochondrial health involves focusing on circadian rhythm, oxidative stress reduction, metabolic stabilization, movement, and deep sleep. When mitochondrial energy rises, hormones become more effective even without changing their levels. Many signs of aging reverse not because hormone levels increase, but because cells regain the energy to respond to those hormones. Aging begins in the mitochondria—and youth returns there as well.

CIRCADIAN RHYTHM COLLAPSE: THE SILENT SABOTEUR

Circadian rhythm is the body's master clock, governing hormone release, neurotransmitter balance, digestion, metabolism, temperature, and sleep cycles. When the circadian system collapses, every downstream hormone becomes desynchronized. Aging accelerates because the timing of internal signals becomes chaotic, even if the hormone levels themselves are not yet dramatically low.

Testosterone production peaks during deep sleep and early morning hours. If melatonin is low or cortisol rises too early, testosterone pulses weaken significantly. This leads to low morning energy, reduced libido, mood instability, and slower muscle repair. Circadian disruption is one of the biggest drivers of early testosterone decline.

Cortisol becomes erratic when circadian timing collapses. Instead of peaking at sunrise, it may peak late at night, causing anxiety, restlessness, and insomnia. Conversely, morning cortisol may be too low, making it difficult to feel alert or motivated. This mistiming produces emotional instability, metabolic resistance, and chronic fatigue.

Estrogen and progesterone rely heavily on circadian cues to regulate receptor sensitivity and metabolic function. When circadian timing is disrupted, estrogen receptors become less responsive. This leads to mood swings, weight gain, and emotional volatility—even when estrogen levels are still relatively normal. For many, symptoms appear long before measurable decline.

Melatonin collapse is both a cause and consequence of circadian disruption. Artificial light at night, irregular sleep, late eating, stress, and poor sleep hygiene all weaken melatonin production. Without melatonin, nighttime cellular repair weakens, increasing aging markers like inflammation, oxidative stress, and mitochondrial dysfunction. A body without circadian alignment ages rapidly.

Growth hormone, thyroid hormones, insulin, and leptin all follow circadian rhythms as well. When the internal clock is misaligned, metabolism becomes resistant, hunger signals become unpredictably strong, and energy regulation falls apart. Circadian collapse is often the first true sign of early biological aging. Fortunately, restoring the rhythm can reverse years of decline within weeks.

THE NERVOUS SYSTEM & HORMONES: HOW STRESS REWIRES AGING

The nervous system and hormonal system are deeply interconnected. Hormones shape how the nervous system responds to stress, emotion, and the environment, while the nervous system influences hormonal output through the hypothalamus and pituitary. When stress becomes chronic, the nervous system shifts into hypervigilance, causing long-term hormonal misalignment.

Cortisol becomes the dominant signal in a stressed nervous system. Over time, this suppresses testosterone, destabilizes estrogen, weakens thyroid function, and disrupts melatonin. The body becomes trapped in sympathetic dominance—the fight-or-flight mode—which prevents proper repair, emotional regulation, and hormonal balance. This is why prolonged stress ages people faster than poor diet or inactivity.

Low testosterone makes the nervous system more sensitive to stress. Testosterone normally acts as a buffer that stabilizes mood and reduces hyper-reactivity. Without it, emotional thresholds lower, irritability increases, and small disruptions feel overwhelming. This amplifies stress further, worsening hormonal decline. The nervous system becomes both the victim and the catalyst.

Low estrogen destabilizes neurotransmitters like serotonin and dopamine, making emotional regulation more difficult. The nervous system becomes more reactive to negative stimuli and less capable of sustaining long-term calm. This creates the internal sensation of "losing resilience," which is often mistakenly attributed to personality changes instead of hormonal shifts.

Melatonin decline reduces the nervous system's ability to enter deep rest states. Without restorative sleep, the parasympathetic nervous system (the "rest-and-digest" system) cannot fully activate. The body becomes trapped in a low-level stress state that suppresses every major hormone. Sleep becomes fragmented, emotional stability deteriorates, and cognitive performance drops.

A dysregulated nervous system alters perception of the world. Stress sensitivity increases, social tolerance decreases, and daily responsibilities feel heavier. These shifts aren't psychological weakness—they are biochemically predictable responses to hormonal imbalance. When nervous system regulation is restored through breathwork, circadian balance, nutrition, and sleep repair, hormones often rebalance naturally.

The nervous system may be the most powerful lever in hormonal restoration. Once it becomes calm and regulated, cortisol stabilizes, melatonin rises, testosterone strengthens, and estrogen receptors regain sensitivity. Nervous system repair often unlocks the fastest visible changes in aging reversal. Hormones cannot align in a body that is stuck in perpetual alertness.

HORMONAL AGING THROUGH SYMPTOMS: THE EARLY WARNING CHECKLIST

Hormonal decline often announces itself long before lab tests reveal abnormalities. The earliest signs are almost always symptomatic, manifesting as shifts in energy, mood, sleep, metabolism, and cognition. These signals form an early warning system that allows you to detect aging long before it becomes biologically entrenched.

One of the most common early signs is morning irritability or difficulty waking. This points to cortisol-melatonin misalignment, reduced testosterone release, or weakened mitochondrial repair. Waking up tired, stiff, or mentally foggy may indicate declining mitochondrial energy rather than poor sleep alone.

Afternoon crashes signal declining cortisol reserves, weakened thyroid function, or low insulin sensitivity. If energy dips sharply around 2–5 p.m., the hormonal system is struggling to regulate metabolic flow. This is an early sign of circadian and adrenal misalignment, often appearing years before major hormonal drops.

Loss of "spark," initiation, or ambition frequently signals low testosterone, unstable dopamine pathways, or weakened estrogen receptor activity. Many people misinterpret this as depression or low self-esteem, but the root is often hormonal. Drive is a biochemical force, not a personality trait.

Brain fog, forgetfulness, or difficulty concentrating reflect melatonin decline, elevated cortisol, mitochondrial stress, or estrogen loss. When cognitive function becomes inconsistent, the hormonal compass is already shifting. The brain relies heavily on hormonal stability for clarity and memory.

Stubborn fat gain—particularly around the abdomen—signals cortisol imbalance, insulin resistance, low estrogen, or low testosterone. When the metabolism becomes resistant, the root cause is almost always hormonal misalignment rather than caloric excess. Hormonal decline changes how the body stores and burns energy.

Sleep fragmentation—waking repeatedly at night, especially between 2–4 a.m.—is a classic sign of cortisol spikes, melatonin suppression, or estrogen fluctuation. Nighttime wakefulness is one of the most accurate predictors of hormonal aging. Restoring sleep often reverses many other symptoms rapidly.

ENVIRONMENTAL HORMONE DISRUPTORS: THE MODERN AGE ACCELERATORS

The modern environment contains hundreds of endocrine-disrupting chemicals (EDCs) that mimic, block, or distort hormonal signals. These chemicals accelerate aging dramatically because they interfere with testosterone, estrogen, thyroid hormones, insulin, and cortisol regulation. Many individuals experience hormonal decline not because of biology, but because of environmental exposure.

Plastics are one of the most significant hormone disruptors. BPA, phthalates, and microplastics mimic estrogen and suppress testosterone. They seep into food, water, and the air. Over time, these synthetic estrogens overwhelm hormone receptors, weaken reproductive hormone production, and increase fat storage. Their impact compounds year after year.

Pesticides introduce estrogenic compounds that accumulate in body fat. These chemicals mimic hormones so effectively that they trick the body into responding incorrectly. This suppresses natural hormone production and destabilizes metabolic signals. Many chronic health issues originate in pesticide exposure long before symptoms appear.

Artificial fragrances are another potent disruptor. Perfumes, scented body products, household cleaners, candles, and air fresheners contain chemical blends that interfere with hormonal balance. These compounds bypass the liver and enter the bloodstream through inhalation, suppressing testosterone, altering cortisol patterns, and weakening thyroid function.

Heavy metals—including mercury, lead, cadmium, and arsenic—damage the endocrine system and disrupt hormone receptors. They impair mitochondrial function, increase oxidative stress, and reduce the body's ability to generate hormones efficiently. Accumulation of these metals accelerates aging through metabolic and neurological pathways.

Blue light from screens is one of the most direct disruptors of melatonin and circadian rhythm. Even small amounts of nighttime exposure suppress melatonin for hours, reducing sleep depth and repair. This alone can accelerate biological aging by increasing oxidative stress and reducing cellular restoration. Technology has become one of the most underestimated aging accelerators.

Water contaminants—including pharmaceuticals, microplastics, and endocrine-disrupting residues—affect hormones on a daily basis. Unfiltered tap water often contains trace amounts of medications, including estrogenic compounds that affect hormonal balance. This contributes to long-term endocrine burden that compounds over years.

THE YOUTHFUL HORMONE SIGNATURE: WHAT BALANCE FEELS LIKE

A youthful hormonal system has a distinct internal signature. It is not defined by perfect lab numbers but by rhythm, stability, clarity, and resilience. Understanding this signature helps readers recognize when their hormonal compass begins realigning.

Youthful hormones create predictable energy. Mornings feel clear and grounded. Midday energy is stable. Evenings bring natural calm without exhaustion. This stability reflects well-timed cortisol, healthy testosterone pulses, and strong melatonin cycles. When hormones are aligned, energy no longer feels chaotic or unpredictable.

Youthful hormonal balance produces emotional resilience. Stress is manageable, irritability is rare, and mood remains steady. This is the result of synchronized cortisol, estrogen, and neurotransmitter activity. Emotional storms become less frequent, and the nervous system remains calm under pressure.

Cognition is sharp with youthful hormones. Memory feels reliable. Focus is consistent. Creativity flows easily. This comes from strong estrogenic signaling, stable cortisol, healthy melatonin, and robust mitochondrial function. The brain feels awake—with no fog or sluggishness.

Metabolism becomes efficient and responsive. The body burns energy smoothly, manages blood sugar well, and maintains stable weight with moderate effort. This reflects balanced insulin, strong thyroid activity, and healthy testosterone or estrogen regulation. Weight loss plateaus disappear, and energy from food becomes predictable.

Sleep becomes deep, restorative, and refreshing. Nighttime wakefulness is rare. Dreams return. Morning energy feels natural. This is melatonin in rhythm, cortisol at its minimum, and the nervous system deeply relaxed. The body begins to repair itself more fully when sleep stabilizes.

A youthful hormonal profile creates a sense of internal alignment. The body feels synchronized, responsive, and alive. This internal signature is the compass that guides you back to hormonal youthfulness. Once recognized, it becomes easier to detect when the system shifts—and easier to restore balance rapidly.

THE INTERNAL MAP: THE HORMONAL COMPASS METAPHOR

Your body operates like a compass with four cardinal hormonal directions. Each direction represents a core hormonal force that governs a different aspect of youth, vitality, and resilience. Understanding these directions helps you interpret your body's signals more accurately.

Testosterone is North—the direction of initiative, strength, drive, and decisive action. When North is strong, you feel capable, assertive, grounded, and confident. When North is weak, you feel directionless, unmotivated, and drained of forward momentum. North is the realm of vitality.

Estrogen is East—the direction of harmony, clarity, intuition, emotional intelligence, and internal balance. When East is aligned, emotions feel stable and relationships flow naturally. When East is disrupted, mood fluctuates, cognitive clarity fades, and stress sensitivity rises. East governs equilibrium.

Cortisol is South—the direction of grounding, survival, alertness, and adaptation. When South is stable, energy remains predictable and focused. When South is chaotic, you become scattered, anxious, fatigued, and overwhelmed. South controls stability under pressure.

Melatonin is West—the direction of rest, repair, dreams, and nightly renewal. When West is strong, you sleep deeply, heal well, and wake restored. When West is weak, sleep becomes fragmented and aging accelerates. West governs regeneration.

When all four directions align—North, East, South, and West—the hormonal compass points toward youth. When one direction weakens, the compass becomes confused, and the body begins drifting toward premature aging. Understanding this internal map empowers you to recognize where your system is misaligned and how to guide it back.

CLOSING REFLECTION

Your hormones are not broken—they are disoriented. Testosterone, estrogen, cortisol, and melatonin form the core of your internal navigation system. When these signals weaken, aging accelerates. When they strengthen, vitality resurfaces. This chapter has shown you the first truth of hormonal youthfulness: decline is not the end of the story. It is a signpost—an opportunity to reorient your internal compass. As you continue through this book, remember that your body has not forgotten how to be young. Its signals simply need to be found again, decoded, and guided back to alignment.

CHAPTER 2 – REBALANCING CYCLES

The importance of light, sleep, and rhythmic living in hormone production

Your hormones do not thrive in chaos. They thrive in rhythm. Light, darkness, temperature shifts, mealtimes, sleep cycles, and daily routines form the invisible scaffolding that supports hormonal balance. Every hormone—testosterone, estrogen, cortisol, melatonin, thyroid hormones, and growth hormone—follows circadian rhythms. These rhythms determine **when** hormones rise, fall, repair, signal, and regulate. When your rhythms collapse, your hormones misfire. When your rhythms strengthen, your body returns to coherence. Rebalancing cycles is not about forcing your hormones—it is about restoring the natural conditions in which they once flourished.

THE RHYTHM OF LIGHT: REALIGNING THE BIOLOGICAL CLOCK

Light is the master conductor of hormonal timing. The moment sunlight touches your eyes in the morning, the brain activates its internal clock and instructs the endocrine system to initiate its daily cycle. This first light exposure determines when cortisol rises, when melatonin stops, when testosterone begins its morning pulse, and when the brain prepares for energy production. Without morning light, the body wakes up chemically confused. Hormones drift. Mood collapses. Metabolism slows. Because modern life traps people indoors, many live in biological darkness—disconnected from the very signal that evolution relied on for millions of years.

Artificial blue light after sunset disrupts these same cycles. Screens mimic daylight frequencies, tricking the brain into thinking it's still daytime. When this happens, melatonin is suppressed for hours, sleep becomes shallow, cortisol rises, and the body's repair signals weaken. This effect compounds night after night, accelerating aging. Evening light pollution is one of the greatest modern disruptors of hormonal health. You cannot generate youthful hormones in an environment that tells your body it is always daytime.

Rebalancing the body begins with controlling light. Morning sunlight anchors the rhythm. Evening darkness completes it. Humans are circadian beings, wired to live within cycles of illumination. When the brain receives consistent light cues, it automatically realigns cortisol, testosterone, growth hormone, thyroid hormones, and insulin. This is why light is not motivational—it is biochemical. Without it, the body becomes hormonally disoriented.

Light also influences mood and neurochemistry. Sunlight increases serotonin, which later transforms into melatonin at night. Bright natural light regulates dopamine, improving motivation and emotional resilience. Dim warm light in the evening activates the parasympathetic nervous system, preparing the body for rest and renewal. The environment becomes the hidden hormone therapy working silently each day.

When you reshape your light environment, your hormones begin correcting themselves without conscious effort. Light is the original medicine for the endocrine system. It is the compass the body has followed for millennia, long before supplements, diets, and modern interventions existed. When you reintroduce natural light cycles, the hormonal system begins to rediscover its natural timing, flow, and intelligence.

EXERCISE SET: LIGHT REBALANCING ROUTINES

Exercise 1 — 10-Minute Morning Sun Reset

1. Immediately after waking, go outside or stand by a window with unobstructed natural light.
2. Look toward (not directly at) the direction of the light.
3. Allow the light to hit your eyes for 10 minutes without sunglasses.
4. Breathe deeply and mentally anchor the moment as your "daily reset."
5. Perform daily to realign cortisol and testosterone rhythms.

Exercise 2 — Sunset Wind-Down Ritual

1. At sunset, dim lights in your home by 50%.
2. Switch to warm lamps, candles, or amber bulbs.
3. Power off screens or shift to night mode.
4. Spend 5 minutes breathing slowly as your body transitions into evening mode.
5. This resets the melatonin clock and preps the endocrine system for night repair.

Exercise 3 — Blue-Light Shield Routine

1. After 8 p.m., eliminate overhead lighting.
2. Wear blue-light blocking glasses if using screens.
3. Reduce screen brightness to its lowest setting.
4. Avoid white/blue LEDs completely.
5. This routine prevents melatonin suppression and restores sleep depth.

THE RHYTHM OF SLEEP: THE NIGHTTIME HORMONAL ENGINE

Sleep is not a luxury—it is a hormone factory. During sleep, your body releases melatonin, repairs mitochondrial DNA, triggers growth hormone pulses, stabilizes cortisol, and produces the early-morning testosterone surge. When sleep is fragmented, late, inconsistent, or shallow, every hormone declines. The body does not just feel tired—it becomes chemically impaired. The endocrine system becomes confused, unable to operate within a stable pattern.

Melatonin is the architect of night cycles. It is released in darkness and suppressed by light, stress, and late eating. Melatonin is not just a sleep hormone—it regulates the timing of almost all other hormone cycles. When melatonin is weak, testosterone drops, cortisol becomes unstable, and estrogen fluctuates unpredictably. Deep sleep stages such as slow-wave sleep and REM require strong melatonin signaling. Without these stages, emotional regulation weakens and metabolic repair stalls.

Growth hormone pulses occur in the first deep sleep window after you fall asleep. If bedtime is late or cortisol is high, this repair window is missed. Growth hormone is responsible for fat loss, muscle repair, collagen production, immune function, and cellular regeneration. Missing this nightly repair cycle accelerates aging. People often think they have a fat-loss problem—but many simply have a sleep-timing problem.

Cortisol and melatonin are opposites. When one rises, the other falls. Proper sleep cycles keep cortisol low at night and high in the morning. When nighttime cortisol rises, the brain cannot enter deep sleep, and melatonin cannot activate. This creates a biochemical inversion that ruins hormonal health. Stress, screens, overstimulation, and nighttime agitation all raise cortisol and suppress melatonin.

Sleep regulates hunger and metabolism. Poor sleep elevates ghrelin (hunger hormone) and destabilizes insulin. This makes cravings stronger, fat storage more aggressive, and energy levels inconsistent. Even the best diets fail when sleep is broken. Hormones require long, consistent sleep cycles to regulate appetite and metabolic function.

A well-calibrated sleep cycle is not just about feeling rested—it is about allowing the endocrine system to follow its natural nightly rhythm. When sleep becomes consistent, predictable, deep, and aligned with circadian biology, hormones self-repair. Night becomes the most powerful hormonal intervention of your entire day.

EXERCISE SET: SLEEP REALIGNMENT ROUTINES

Exercise 1 — The 90-Minute Sleep Window Reset

1. Choose a consistent bedtime.
2. Allow at least 90 minutes before bed with no screens.
3. Dim lights and transition to warm lighting.
4. Avoid food for 2–3 hours before bed.
5. Start lowering activity gradually.
   This trains the brain to enter predictable melatonin release.

Exercise 2 — The Pre-Sleep Nervous System Drop

1. Sit on your bed with your back supported.
2. Inhale for 4 seconds, exhale for 8 seconds.
3. Repeat for 2–3 minutes.
4. Keep eyes half-lidded to activate parasympathetic pathways.
5. This technique lowers nighttime cortisol.

Exercise 3 — Morning Wake Ritual to Lock the Cycle

1. Wake at the same time daily, even on weekends.
2. Drink water immediately to signal liver/hormonal activation.
3. Get 5–10 minutes of light exposure.
4. Move your body for 60 seconds (stretch or walk).
5. This locks the internal 24-hour clock into place.

THE RHYTHM OF DAILY LIVING: MEALS, MOVEMENT & INTERNAL TIMING

Daily rhythms determine how hormones flow throughout the day. Hormones require predictability, not perfection. The brain needs cues for when to raise energy, when to rest, when to digest, and when to repair. Unpredictable schedules confuse the endocrine system. Late meals, erratic wake times, skipped breakfasts, emotional upheavals, and inconsistent movement patterns disrupt the hormonal rhythm. Reestablishing daily cycles rewires the endocrine system into stability.

Meal timing has a profound impact on hormonal balance. Eating meals at consistent times stabilizes insulin, reduces cortisol spikes, and improves testosterone and estrogen sensitivity. A predictable eating window reduces metabolic confusion and reduces inflammation. Eating at irregular times, especially late at night, shifts the body into constant stress signaling. The digestive system needs a break at night—it was never designed for 24-hour feeding.

Movement rhythms also matter. Morning movement raises cortisol appropriately, improves dopamine function, and activates testosterone. Midday movement increases metabolic flexibility and supports estrogen stability. Evening movement should be gentle to avoid raising cortisol too late in the day. The endocrine system responds differently depending on the time of day. Synchronizing movement with hormone cycles magnifies results.

Rest rhythms are equally important. Midday breaks, deep breathing, and slow moments restore parasympathetic balance. Without breaks, cortisol climbs steadily throughout the day. Even a 3-minute rest ritual can reset the entire system. The nervous system prefers oscillation—periods of effort followed by intentional stillness. This oscillation prevents stress accumulation and supports hormonal harmony.

Internal temperature rhythms affect hormones as well. The body cools at night to trigger melatonin production. Hot showers at night may interfere with melatonin unless followed by a cooldown. Conversely, warm exposure during the day increases metabolic signaling. Understanding temperature rhythms helps restore natural endocrine flow.

When daily rhythms are consistent—wake time, sunlight exposure, meals, movement, rest, and bedtime—the body shifts into a hormonal coherence state. Many symptoms of imbalance disappear not because you force hormones to change, but because you remove internal chaos. Rhythm is the mother-language of hormones.

EXERCISE SET: DAILY RHYTHM REALIGNMENT

Exercise 1 — The Hormonal Meal Anchor

1. Choose a consistent time for your first meal.
2. Eat protein + healthy fats (not sugar).
3. Avoid eating within 2 hours of bedtime.
4. Anchor meals at predictable times each day.
5. Watch energy, mood, and hunger stabilize in one week.

Exercise 2 — 3-Minute Midday Reset

1. Sit or stand still.
2. Inhale for 4 seconds, hold for 2, exhale for 6.
3. Relax the jaw, shoulders, and stomach.
4. Repeat for 3 minutes.
5. This resets cortisol and improves afternoon hormonal equilibrium.

Exercise 3 — Evening Rhythm Lock-In

1. Shut off overhead lights after sunset.
2. Engage in slow movement: walking or stretching.
3. Set tomorrow's intention to calm the mind.
4. Avoid stimulating conversation or conflict.
5. This anchors the brain into nighttime hormonal mode.

CLOSING REFLECTION

Your body is not just a biochemical machine—it is a rhythmic organism. Every hormone you produce follows cycles of light and darkness, wakefulness and rest, eating and fasting, motion and stillness. When life becomes chaotic, your endocrine system loses rhythm. But when you return to predictable cycles, your hormones come home. Chapter 2 teaches a simple truth: **hormonal healing begins with rhythm.** Light sets the compass. Sleep repairs the engine. Daily routines stabilize the flow. When you reclaim your cycles, your hormones stop fighting for survival and begin moving in harmony again. You are not rebuilding your body—you are returning it to the rhythm it always knew.

CHAPTER 3 – ADAPTOGEN ALCHEMY

How to use herbs like ashwagandha, maca, and rhodiola to rebuild your endocrine flow

Your endocrine system is a living symphony, and adaptogenic herbs are the conductors that help restore harmony when signals weaken, drift, or destabilize. Adaptogens do not force hormones; they **teach** hormones. They train your nervous system, mitochondria, and endocrine glands to return to equilibrium under stress. Unlike stimulants—short, sharp, draining—adaptogens are rhythmic, intelligent, and stabilizing. They nourish the adrenal glands, support thyroid flow, balance reproductive hormones, and stabilize the stress axis. Chapter 3 explores the three master adaptogens—**ashwagandha**, **maca**, and **rhodiola**—each with a unique biochemical personality and energetic signature. Together, they form a powerful triad capable of enhancing hormonal resilience, emotional strength, and long-term vitality.

ASHWAGANDHA: THE ADRENAL RESTORER

Ashwagandha is one of the most powerful adaptogens for restoring the adrenal glands and rebalancing cortisol. It lowers nighttime cortisol, reduces anxiety, deepens sleep, and protects the nervous system from chronic overactivation. What makes ashwagandha unique is its dual action: it calms an overstimulated body *and* strengthens an exhausted one. This yin-yang effect is why it is often called "the herb of total restoration." It signals to the HPA axis (the stress-control center in the brain) that the environment is safe again, allowing the endocrine system to shift out of survival mode and back into balanced flow.

Biochemically, ashwagandha increases GABA activity, reduces oxidative stress in adrenal tissues, and supports thyroid hormone conversion—particularly the activation of T3, the hormone that drives metabolic energy. In testosterone pathways, ashwagandha indirectly enhances androgen production by lowering chronic cortisol that competes for shared biochemical precursors. This results in improved libido, deeper sleep, stronger mood stability, and enhanced recovery. It is not merely calming—it reawakened the body's ability to regulate itself.

Energetically, ashwagandha grounds the nervous system. It stabilizes emotional storms, quiets internal agitation, and softens the tension that disrupts endocrine flow. Many people live with low-grade internal panic without realizing it; ashwagandha dissolves that background noise. It is especially powerful for those experiencing burnout, insomnia, chronic stress, emotional exhaustion, or adrenal depletion.

Ashwagandha's strength comes from consistency. Its effects compound over days and weeks, creating deep changes in hormonal rhythms. Taken at night, it enhances melatonin release. Taken in the morning, it stabilizes cortisol. Taken long-term, it rebuilds nervous system resilience. This herb does not just support hormones—it supports the terrain in which hormones operate.

Adaptogen alchemy with ashwagandha is about creating a daily ritual that signals safety, grounding, and internal recalibration. Its power is subtle, but its effect is profound: calmer nights, steadier days, balanced stress responses, and a body that stops burning energy in the background.

RECIPES — ASHWAGANDHA

Recipe 1 — Ashwagandha Ghee Moon Milk

Ingredients:

- 1 cup warm almond or oat milk
- 1 teaspoon ashwagandha powder
- 1 teaspoon ghee
- ½ teaspoon cinnamon
- 1 teaspoon honey
- Pinch nutmeg

Instructions:

Warm milk on low heat. Stir in ashwagandha, ghee, cinnamon, and nutmeg until dissolved. Add honey last.

Benefits: Deep sleep, cortisol reduction, nighttime hormonal reset.

Recipe 2 — Ashwagandha Stress-Lowering Tea

Ingredients:

- 1 cup hot water
- ½–1 teaspoon ashwagandha powder
- 1 ginger tea bag (store-bought is fine)
- 1 teaspoon lemon juice

Steep ginger tea, then add ashwagandha and lemon.

Benefits: Combines the universal endocrine support of ginger with the adrenal repair of ashwagandha.

Recipe 3 — Ashwagandha Chocolate Power Bites

Ingredients:

- 2 tablespoons cacao powder
- 1 tablespoon ashwagandha
- 1 tablespoon honey
- 1 tablespoon almond butter
- Pinch sea salt

Mix, form small bites, refrigerate.

Benefits: A calm-energy snack that stabilizes cortisol and nourishes hormonal pathways.

MACA: THE REPRODUCTIVE AMPLIFIER

Maca is known as the endocrine elevator—an adaptogen specializing in the reproductive axis. It does not contain hormones itself; instead, it nourishes the hypothalamus and pituitary, the two master glands that regulate estrogen, testosterone, progesterone, and growth hormone. Maca revitalizes libido, stabilizes menstrual rhythms, strengthens androgen pathways, and boosts overall reproductive vitality. Its power lies in its ability to nourish—not stimulate—the endocrine system.

Biochemically, maca increases dopamine sensitivity, enhances nitric oxide production, and supports the body's natural estrogen/testosterone balance. For individuals with low testosterone, maca can improve energy, libido, and mental clarity. For individuals with declining estrogen or irregular cycles, maca can smooth emotional fluctuations, reduce PMS symptoms, and support reproductive hormone flow. It adjusts according to the body's needs, not in a single direction.

Maca's nutrient profile is one of the richest of all roots. It contains amino acids, B vitamins, magnesium, iron, potassium, and plant sterols that serve as hormonal precursors. This makes maca deeply restorative during hormonal transitions—perimenopause, stress-induced imbalance, post-burnout recovery, and reproductive fatigue.

Energetically, maca is warming, uplifting, and strengthening. It boosts vitality without overstimulation and restores sexual energy without creating nervous system strain. It improves mood, motivation, and physical stamina, making it an ideal adaptogen for those who feel emotionally flat, fatigued, or hormonally depleted.

Unlike caffeine, maca elevates energy without taxing the adrenals. Its slow, consistent effect makes it ideal for morning or midday use. When taken regularly, it improves androgen sensitivity, stabilizes estrogenic rhythms, and deepens the body's internal vitality.

Maca is an adaptogen of empowerment—restoring the parts of you that feel dimmed, drained, or disconnected. It reawakens internal fire, reproductive vitality, and hormonal flow.

RECIPES — MACA

Recipe 1 — Maca Morning Hormone Smoothie

Ingredients:

- 1 banana
- 1 teaspoon maca
- 1 tablespoon almond butter
- ½ cup blueberries
- 1 cup almond milk

Blend and drink in the morning.

Benefits: Supports testosterone, estrogen, dopamine, and metabolic flow.

Recipe 2 — Maca Golden Ghee Latte

Ingredients:

- 1 teaspoon maca
- 1 teaspoon turmeric
- 1 tablespoon ghee
- 1 cup warm milk
- Honey to taste

Warm milk with turmeric and ghee. Stir in maca.

Benefits: Hormonal-stabilizing fats + endocrine-nourishing maca = morning hormonal ignition.

Recipe 3 — Maca Chocolate Libido Booster

Ingredients:

- 1 tablespoon maca
- 1 tablespoon cacao
- ½ teaspoon cinnamon
- Hot water or milk
- Honey

Mix into a warm drink.

Benefits: Enhances libido, mood, reproductive vitality.

RHODIOLA: THE ENERGY STABILIZER

Rhodiola is the adaptogen of resilience, stamina, and cognitive clarity. It supports mitochondrial energy, stabilizes dopamine and serotonin, and strengthens the body's capacity to handle stress without crashing. Rhodiola does not sedate; it sharpens. It is the adaptogen for individuals who feel burned out, unfocused, overwhelmed, or mentally taxed.

Biochemically, rhodiola increases oxygen utilization, enhances ATP production, and protects neurons from stress-induced fatigue. It is particularly effective for individuals with stress-related exhaustion, midday crashes, low motivation, brain fog, or emotional volatility. Rhodiola strengthens the adrenal glands but also helps prevent overstimulation. It is energizing yet balanced—a rare combination.

Rhodiola is a master regulator of cortisol timing. It reduces excess cortisol when high, increases production when low, and stabilizes its rhythm when erratic. This makes it an ideal herb for individuals with chaotic stress responses or a history of prolonged burnout. Its ability to regulate the stress axis helps the endocrine system follow predictable rhythms again.

Energetically, rhodiola opens mental clarity, restores stamina, and brings resilience back online. It supports strong emotional centers, improves motivation, and strengthens the capacity to handle life's pressures. Unlike stimulants, which "borrow energy," rhodiola builds internal reserves. People feel more present, more capable, and more grounded.

Rhodiola also supports serotonin pathways, making it highly effective for stress-induced mood imbalances, seasonal depression, and emotional flattening. It increases mental endurance and reduces cognitive fatigue—key for rebuilding the endocrine system after prolonged stress.

This herb is best taken in the morning or early afternoon because of its energizing nature. With daily use, rhodiola strengthens stress resilience, boosts energy, enhances hormonal clarity, and brings the body out of survival mode into sustainable vitality.

RECIPES — RHODIOLA

Recipe 1 — Rhodiola Morning Clarity Tea

Ingredients:

- 1 rhodiola tea bag or ½ teaspoon powdered rhodiola
- 1 cup hot water
- ½ teaspoon honey
- Small slice of lemon

Steep for 4–6 minutes.

Benefits: Improves mental clarity, energizes without overstimulation, stabilizes cortisol.

Recipe 2 — Rhodiola Energy Elixir Smoothie

Ingredients:

- ½ teaspoon rhodiola
- 1 cup coconut water
- ½ cup strawberries
- 1 teaspoon chia seeds
- Ice

Blend until chilled.

Benefits: Supports ATP production, hydration, adrenal rhythm, and emotional clarity.

Recipe 3 — Rhodiola Adaptogenic Iced Tea

Ingredients:

- 2 cups brewed rhodiola tea (from powder or tea bags)
- 1 tablespoon lemon juice
- ½ teaspoon ginger (powder or fresh)
- Ice
- Optional: mint

Mix and pour over ice.

Benefits: Cooling, stress-lowering, focus-enhancing tonic.

CLOSING REFLECTION

Adaptogens are not magic—they are teachers. They show your endocrine system how to respond to stress, how to regulate flow, how to restore rhythm, and how to return to balance. Ashwagandha grounds the body into calm and replenishes the stress axis. Maca lifts the reproductive system and restores vitality. Rhodiola sharpens the mind and fortifies resilience. Together, these herbs create an alchemy that reawakens your hormonal intelligence. When taken consistently, respectfully, and rhythmically, adaptogens help your body remember what balanced hormones feel like. Healing does not need force—only guidance. These herbs are the guides.

CHAPTER 4 – THE SOLAR PULSE

Why timing your movement and meals to sunlight restores hormonal harmony

Your body is not designed to operate on a constant schedule created by modern society—it is designed to operate on **light**. Every endocrine signal inside you responds to the rising and setting of the sun. The pulse of daylight sets the rhythm of cortisol, testosterone, estrogen, thyroid output, appetite hormones, and melatonin. When you align your movement and meals with sunlight, your hormones no longer work against you—they begin to flow in harmony with nature's original timing system. The sun becomes a metronome that restores metabolic balance, sharpens energy, and resets circadian pathways that have been lost through years of artificial living. The Solar Pulse is not merely about sunlight—it is about remembering the ancient pattern your biology never forgot.

WHY THE BODY NEEDS SOLAR-TIMED MOVEMENT

The human body evolved outdoors, in sync with dawn brightness and sunset dimming. Movement during sunlight is not optional—it is genetic. When you move in sunlight, photons hit the eyes and skin, triggering hormonal cascades: cortisol rises in the morning to energize you; testosterone strengthens during daylight-triggered activity; growth hormone pulses after sunlight-exposed exercise. Midday light boosts serotonin, allowing melatonin to form later in the evening. Modern life broke this cycle. Indoor living creates hormonal drift and metabolic chaos, leaving the body uncertain about when to activate or rest.

Morning sunlight movement sends the strongest circadian signal to the brain, telling it: *"It is time to produce energy, burn fat, and wake the metabolic system."* This strengthens cortisol rhythm, stabilizes blood sugar, and improves thyroid function. When the body moves outdoors early in the day, the adrenal glands release cortisol in the proper pattern—high in the morning, low at night—preventing insomnia, anxiety, and nighttime cravings. Without sunlight movement, cortisol becomes erratic, creating hormonal confusion.

Movement timed to solar cycles also regulates reproductive hormones. Testosterone increases when exercise aligns with sunlight, especially within the first four hours after waking. Estrogen stabilizes through improved blood flow and temperature regulation. Even insulin becomes more predictable when movement happens during daylight. Your hormones read sunlight as a signal of safety, allowing the body to spend energy efficiently rather than storing it defensively.

The endocrine system also depends on temperature shifts created by early morning coolness and midday warmth. Movement in cool sunlight triggers brown fat activation and metabolic efficiency. Movement in warm sunlight increases blood flow, oxygenation, and lymphatic circulation. Each temperature environment supports a different hormonal outcome, giving the body cues for rebuilding or releasing energy.

Solar movement also regulates dopamine. Exercise in daylight increases dopamine receptor density, improving motivation, drive, creativity, and focus. Without sunlight, dopamine becomes sluggish, making tasks feel harder, heavier, and more draining. This is why indoor exercise often feels less energizing than outdoor movement—the hormones are not aligned properly.

When movement follows the Solar Pulse, the body stops fighting itself. Energy becomes predictable, mood stabilizes, appetite aligns with natural hunger patterns, and sleep deepens. The sun becomes your biological "on switch," training your endocrine system to behave like it was designed to: rhythmic, stable, and powerful.

EXERCISE SET — SOLAR MOVEMENT ROUTINES

Exercise 1 — The 10-Minute Dawn Activation Walk

1. Go outside within 30–60 minutes of waking.
2. Walk slowly or briskly for 10 minutes—no headphones, no screens.
3. Let sunlight hit your face and gaze toward the horizon.
4. Allow your breath to sync with your steps.
5. This anchors cortisol and testosterone timing for the entire day.

Exercise 2 — Midday Solar Strength Reset

1. Step outdoors sometime between 11 a.m. and 2 p.m.
2. Do 3–5 minutes of gentle strength movements:
   - Bodyweight squats
   - Push-ups against a wall
   - Slow lunges
3. Let the bright light increase serotonin and thyroid activity.
4. Use slow, controlled breaths to activate the parasympathetic system.
5. This boosts afternoon energy without caffeine.

Exercise 3 — Sunset Wind-Down Stretch Flow

1. At sunset, go outside or near an open window.
2. Perform gentle stretches: forward fold, hip openers, chest expansion.
3. Breathe deeply while watching the light fade.
4. Allow your nervous system to shift into nighttime mode.
5. This lowers cortisol and initiates melatonin production.

WHY MEAL TIMING MUST FOLLOW THE SUNLIGHT MAP

Your digestive system is tied to sunlight just as much as your endocrine system. Hormones that regulate hunger, metabolism, and fat storage follow a circadian rhythm. Ghrelin (hunger hormone) rises naturally in the morning. Insulin sensitivity peaks at midday. Digestive enzymes are most active when sunlight is strong. Eating late at night disrupts these rhythms and forces the body to digest during its repair window, sabotaging melatonin and increasing cortisol. Solar-timed eating restores metabolic flow and hormonal harmony.

When you eat your first meal in alignment with sunlight—after hydration, light exposure, and gentle movement—the body reads it as a controlled metabolic event. Insulin behaves predictably, cortisol remains in balance, and blood sugar stabilizes. Skipping breakfast entirely can work for some, but only if sunlight exposure is strong and cortisol is regulated. Eating in darkness, however, always disrupts hormones. Meals anchored to sunlight stabilize hunger signals and reduce cravings driven by circadian confusion rather than true need.

Midday is the body's metabolic peak. This is when digestive heat, enzyme production, and insulin sensitivity are highest. Eating your largest meal during this window supports thyroid function, reproductive hormone balance, and stable energy. When the biggest meal is pushed to nighttime, the endocrine system misfires: insulin spikes, melatonin drops, cortisol rises, and fat storage increases. This is not dieting—it is circadian biology.

Evening eating should be light, warm, and calming. Heavy or late meals disrupt melatonin and delay the beginning of cellular repair. Hormones cannot rise properly when the digestive system is still working. Light dinners reduce inflammation, protect sleep, and improve hormonal repair cycles. This gives the endocrine system a clear signal: *"Night mode engaged."*

Solar-timed meals also reduce stress on the liver. The liver processes hormones, detoxifies estrogen, regulates thyroid conversion, and stabilizes blood sugar. When food is consumed in rhythm with sunlight, the liver becomes more efficient. Hormonal fluctuations become smoother, emotional stability improves, and energy remains consistent.

Meal timing is not about deprivation—it is about restoring the natural endocrine timing that makes your body work with you instead of against you. When you eat in alignment with sunlight, you return your metabolism to its original design: efficient, energetic, and hormonally balanced.

EXERCISE SET — SOLAR EATING ROUTINES

Exercise 1 — Sunlit First Meal Ritual

1. Hydrate first (water, ginger tea, or lemon water).
2. Get light exposure before eating.
3. Eat a protein + healthy fat first meal (no sugar).
4. Keep the first meal within the first 2–4 hours after waking.
5. This stabilizes cortisol, insulin, and appetite hormones.

Exercise 2 — Midday Metabolic Peak Meal

1. Schedule your largest or most nutrient-dense meal between 11 a.m.–2 p.m.
2. Include protein, vegetables, and a slow carb.
3. Eat without rushing or multitasking.
4. Sit in a sunlit room or go outdoors afterward for 5 minutes.
5. This maximizes thyroid and reproductive hormone support.

Exercise 3 — Sunset Light Dinner Protocol

1. Avoid eating 2–3 hours before bed.
2. Choose warm, simple foods: soups, broths, cooked vegetables.
3. Dim lights while eating to lower cortisol.
4. Sip a calming herbal tea (ginger, lemon balm, chamomile).
5. This signals to the brain that melatonin should rise naturally.

HOW SOLAR ALIGNMENT REWIRES THE ENDOCRINE SYSTEM

When you align your movement and meals with sunlight, the endocrine system begins to reorganize itself. Cortisol becomes predictable: high in the morning, low at night. Testosterone rises during morning and midday activity. Estrogen stabilizes due to improved blood flow, metabolic timing, and consistent sleep cycles. Thyroid hormones improve due to temperature regulation and circadian alignment. Insulin sensitivity increases, reducing inflammation and stabilizing weight. Melatonin deepens because you stop sending mixed signals to your internal clock.

Your mitochondria—the engines of your cells—respond directly to solar patterns. Morning light improves mitochondrial energy production. Midday movement increases oxygen use and ATP output. Evening dimness allows mitochondria to switch into repair mode. This creates a 24-hour cycle of peak energy and deep restoration. Hormones depend on mitochondrial rhythms; when mitochondria run smoothly, hormonal signals regain clarity.

The nervous system also reorganizes. Solar alignment reduces sympathetic dominance (fight-or-flight) and increases parasympathetic activity (rest-and-digest). This reduces chronic cortisol, protects adrenal health, and improves emotional stability. Stress responses become smoother. Anxiety reduces. Overwhelm decreases. Rhythmic living rewires the emotional center of the brain.

Even digestion shifts into harmony. Solar-timed meals improve gut motility, enzyme production, microbiome balance, and nutrient absorption. The gut produces neurotransmitters and interacts constantly with hormones. When the gut follows sunlight, emotional and hormonal stability improve.

Over time, the entire hormonal system begins to operate like a well-tuned instrument—predictable, responsive, and stable. Instead of forcing hormones through supplements or guesswork, you restore the foundation on which they depend. Light becomes your therapy. Timing becomes your medicine. Rhythm becomes your power.

The Solar Pulse does not ask you to change your entire life—it asks you to change the timing of your life. When timed correctly, even small habits create profound hormonal transformation.

CLOSING REFLECTION

Your hormones are not random—they are rhythmic. They rise and fall with the sun, the temperature, and the flow of your daily actions. When you live in alignment with sunlight, your body comes back into its natural intelligence. Hormones stop fighting. Mood stabilizes. Energy smooths. Hunger becomes predictable. Sleep deepens. The Solar Pulse is not about discipline—it is about returning to the ancient timing encoded into your DNA. You do not create harmony; **you return to it**. And with each sunrise and sunset, your endocrine system begins to remember the rhythm it was born to follow.

CHAPTER 5 — THE COMPASS RITUAL

Create a daily sunrise or sunset ritual to lock in hormonal alignment

There is a moment each day when everything becomes still. The world pauses between light and darkness, and your internal compass becomes the most sensitive, the most open, and the most able to realign. That moment—the rising sun or the falling sun—is where your body's hormonal rhythm receives its strongest signal. The endocrine system listens for that shift in light: cortisol calibrates, melatonin rises or retreats, testosterone and estrogen adjust their flow, and the nervous system transitions between day mode and night mode. The Compass Ritual takes advantage of this biological doorway. It transforms sunrise or sunset into a sacred reset point that locks your hormones into rhythm, guides your energy, and restores your internal timing.

The Compass Ritual works because it aligns your brain, skin, breath, and emotions with the Earth's natural transition point. At sunrise, the ritual awakens your cortisol curve, boosts dopamine and serotonin, strengthens testosterone signaling, and primes the thyroid for metabolic daytime function. At sunset, the ritual dissolves cortisol, activates melatonin, grounds the nervous system, and signals the body to begin deep hormonal repair. The ritual itself is not complex—its power lies in consistency and timing. Hormones respond to repetition. When your body learns that each sunrise or sunset contains a specific sequence of breath, stillness, and light exposure, it begins reorganizing itself around that rhythmic anchor.

This ritual also creates a psychological boundary between the frantic pace of daily life and the calm flow of endocrine alignment. The mind quiets differently during transitions of light. Worries soften. Clarity increases. Emotional static clears. You feel yourself land back into your body. Hormonal healing is just as much about recalibrating the nervous system as it is about balancing biochemical pathways, and the Compass Ritual does both at once. It brings coherence where there was chaos. Stillness where there was adrenaline. Orientation where there was confusion.

The Compass Ritual is adaptable: it can be performed at sunrise *or* sunset, depending on your life rhythm. Sunrise reinforces daytime hormones and metabolic activation; sunset reinforces nighttime hormones and restorative cycles. Performing both creates the strongest circadian alignment possible, but performing one consistently becomes the anchor for your endocrine compass. You decide which version serves you best.

The ritual is divided into six phases: **Arrival, Light Activation, Breath Sequencing, Grounding, Hormonal Intention Setting, and Closing Integration.** Each phase communicates with your body in a different language—light, breath, temperature, posture, and inner focus. Each phase has a direct hormonal impact. The ritual becomes more than a habit; it becomes a compass that recalibrates you toward your center every single day.

Below is the full detailed ritual. This is the closing gift of the book: your daily hormonal alignment practice. When you practice it consistently, you are no longer merely managing hormones—you are commanding them.

THE FULL COMPASS RITUAL

A Daily Sunrise or Sunset Practice to Lock in Hormonal Harmony

PHASE 1 — ARRIVAL: SETTING THE INTERNAL COMPASS

1. Step outside or stand by an open window facing the direction of the sun.
2. Pause before doing anything. Let your body feel the air, temperature, and stillness.
3. Place one hand on your chest and one on your lower abdomen.
4. Whisper internally: **"I am here."**
5. Allow your brain to register that this is a moment of transition.
   Hormonal impact: The nervous system drops into parasympathetic awareness; cortisol stabilizes; the body prepares to receive a circadian signal.

PHASE 2 — LIGHT ACTIVATION: SIGNALING YOUR HORMONE CLOCK

1. Look toward (not directly at) the sunlight for 30–60 seconds.
2. Allow natural light to enter your eyes—no sunglasses.
3. Feel warmth or brightness touch your skin.
4. Keep your neck relaxed and your breath open.
5. Stay still and simply receive.
   Hormonal impact:
   • Sunrise version: cortisol rises appropriately, testosterone awakens, thyroid activity increases.
   • Sunset version: melatonin begins to rise, cortisol falls, adrenal tension melts.

PHASE 3 — BREATH SEQUENCING: CLEARING THE HORMONAL PATHWAYS

1. Inhale for 4 seconds.
2. Hold for 2 seconds.
3. Exhale for 6–8 seconds.
4. Repeat 10–15 cycles, slow and smooth.
5. Keep eyes soft and jaw relaxed.

   Hormonal impact: Long exhales lower cortisol, stabilize the stress axis, and deepen parasympathetic activation. Breath becomes the bridge between emotion and hormone.

PHASE 4 — GROUNDING: RETURNING TO THE BODY'S ORIGINAL FREQUENCY

1. Place both feet flat on the ground—barefoot if possible.
2. Imagine your weight dropping into your heels.
3. Visualize the Earth pulling excess cortisol out of your body.
4. Gently roll your shoulders back and open your chest.
5. Breathe as if your feet are inhaling for you.

   Hormonal impact: Grounding reduces adrenal overactivation, improves melatonin regulation, calms the immune system, and promotes testosterone and estrogen balance.

PHASE 5 — HORMONAL INTENTION SETTING: DIRECTING THE COMPASS

Choose **one** intention depending on sunrise vs sunset:

Sunrise Intentions (Daytime Hormones):

- "Let my energy rise in alignment with the light."
- "Let my mind stay clear and focused."
- "Let my hormones support strength, vitality, and clarity today."

Sunset Intentions (Nighttime Hormones):

- "Let my body enter healing."
- "Let my mind release the weight of the day."
- "Let my hormones reset in peace and safety."

Say it silently or aloud.

Hormonal impact: Intention directs perception; perception alters cortisol, dopamine, serotonin, and melatonin pathways. You become the signal.

PHASE 6 — CLOSING INTEGRATION: LOCKING IN THE RITUAL

1. Place both hands over the center of your chest.
2. Take one final inhale through the nose.
3. Exhale through the mouth slowly.
4. Whisper internally: **"Alignment activated."**
5. Turn away from the sun slowly and re-enter your day or night.
   Hormonal impact: This final step anchors the ritual in memory, helping the brain recognize it as the "official transition," ensuring your endocrine system follows the compass you just set.

CLOSING REFLECTION

This is the ritual that brings everything together.

The science.

The cycles.

The adaptogens.

The hormones.

The stress axis.

Your body's natural intelligence.

The Compass Ritual is your doorway into daily hormonal coherence. It draws on the oldest rhythm of life—the rising and falling sun—to teach your body how to function in harmony again. You do not force cortisol or testosterone or melatonin into balance; you show them where to stand. You teach them their timing. You give them their map.

Every time you perform this ritual, you remind your body:

Here is where the day begins.

Here is where the night begins.

Here is where I realign.

And the endocrine system listens.

Every single time.

FINAL EPILOGUE MESSAGE

When your hormones remember who you are, your body does too.

There comes a moment in every healing journey when something begins to shift—not in your mind, not in your habits, but in the silent architecture of your body. It is subtle at first. A deeper inhale. A steadier morning. A calmer evening. A quieter mind. A sense that your energy is no longer scattering outward in all directions, but returning home to you. This moment is not random; it is the moment your hormones begin to remember your true rhythm. That remembrance is sacred. It means your body is no longer fighting for survival—it is rediscovering who you are beneath the chaos, beneath the stress, beneath the versions of you shaped by exhaustion rather than intention.

Your hormones are storytellers. For years, they have carried the imprint of your pace, your fears, your overextension, your sleeplessness, and your struggles. They have mirrored your environment, your emotions, your choices, and your burdens. But they have also carried your resilience. They have carried your potential. They have carried the blueprint of harmony that once guided your childhood body—the body that knew how to wake with ease, how to sleep with depth, how to digest, recover, rebuild, and thrive without effort. That wisdom never left. It simply went quiet beneath the noise of modern living.

Throughout this journey, you have not merely adjusted habits—you have rewritten your internal timing. You have shown your body when to rise, when to rest, when to open, when to repair. You have spoken the language your hormones understand: light, breath, rhythm, nourishment, intention. You've given your body something it has been missing for years—consistency, clarity, and cues. That is why you feel different. That is why things are shifting. Hormones respond to truth, and you have finally returned their truth to them.

This book was never about perfection. It was never about chasing youth or forcing change. It was about alignment. It was about remembering the way your body was designed to move through the world—with fluidity, with presence, with instinctive intelligence. Each ritual, each rhythm, each practice has been a compass pointing you back to yourself. And with every sunrise and sunset, that compass grows steadier. Your hormones have begun their return, and with them, your vitality follows.

As you move forward, remember this:

Your body is not your enemy.

Your hormones are not broken.

Your energy is not gone.

Everything you thought you lost is still within you, waiting for rhythm to call it forth again.

When your hormones remember who you are, your body does too.

And once the body remembers, it rebuilds.

Once it rebuilds, it restores.

Once it restores, it transforms.

You are now living from a place of alignment—not force.

You are not chasing balance anymore.

You are *becoming* it.

This is the beginning of your new rhythm.

Walk forward with it.

Live in partnership with it.

Let your hormones guide you back into the fullness of who you were always meant to be.

Your compass is no longer lost.

It's pointing home.

APPENDIX A

THE COMPASS VISUALIZATION | DAILY ENDOCRINE AFFIRMATIONS | CANDLE + BREATH COMPASS RESET RITUAL

Your endocrine system responds not only to light, movement, food, and sleep—it also responds to imagery, breath, emotion, and inner intention. Visualization, spoken affirmations, and symbolic rituals create subtle biochemical shifts that reinforce everything you have built in the previous chapters. Appendix Â is a three-part daily toolkit designed to reinforce hormonal alignment in minutes.

You can perform each tool separately, or combine all three for a deeper daily ritual.

SECTION 1 — THE COMPASS VISUALIZATION

A guided imagery sequence to realign your hormonal flow

This visualization is best performed during sunrise or sunset, or anytime you feel your body drifting into stress, fatigue, emotional heaviness, or hormonal fog. It resets your internal compass using breath, imagery, and directional intention.

THE VISUALIZATION

Close your eyes and bring your awareness to the center of your chest. Imagine this space as the point where all your inner directions meet. This is your internal compass—quiet, glowing, steady. Take a slow inhale and visualize a soft golden light rising inside your chest, as if the sun itself has awakened within you. Feel warmth spread through your ribs, shoulders, and spine. Let this light represent clarity, stability, and hormonal harmony.

Now imagine four beams of light extending outward from your chest like compass points. Each direction represents a major hormone cycle.

East symbolizes cortisol and awakening energy.

South symbolizes testosterone and inner power.

West symbolizes melatonin and restorative healing.

North symbolizes estrogen, intuition, and emotional balance.

See these four beams of light expanding outward, connecting you to the natural world. Imagine these beams aligning perfectly, forming a balanced, radiant cross of directions. Let them rotate slowly until they lock into place—your internal compass finding its true orientation.

As the compass locks, visualize your hormones shifting into their optimal rhythms. Cortisol rises smoothly with the sun. Testosterone strengthens your core and confidence. Estrogen flows in emotional steadiness. Melatonin deepens in silence. You feel your entire endocrine system become synchronized, coordinated, and responsive. The chaos dissolves. Only clarity remains.

Take one final inhale, imagining the compass drawing back into your chest, glowing like a golden ember. Whisper inwardly: **"Aligned."** Open your eyes gently, carrying this internal alignment into your day or night.

SECTION 2 — DAILY ENDOCRINE AFFIRMATIONS

Hormone-alignment affirmations spoken in the language of biological rhythm

Affirmations are not merely emotional—they influence breath, nervous system tone, cortisol pacing, and the internal narrative your hormones respond to. These daily endocrine affirmations reprogram your emotional biofield and energetic posture so your hormones can follow.

Speak them aloud or silently.

MORNING ENDORCRINE AFFIRMATIONS

Use these during sunrise, morning movement, or your first light exposure.

- **"My energy rises with the sun, naturally and easily."**
- **"My cortisol supports me; it does not control me."**
- **"My hormones move in rhythm with clarity and purpose."**
- **"I welcome strength, focus, and grounded vitality."**
- **"My body knows exactly how to begin the day."**

MIDDAY AFFIRMATIONS

Use these before or after your largest meal, or during a midday reset.

- **"My metabolism is strong, steady, and responsive."**
- **"My endocrine system adapts with intelligence."**
- **"I move through the day with stamina and intention."**
- **"My hormones support consistent mood and energy."**

EVENING AFFIRMATIONS

Use these at sunset, before your night routine, or before bed.

- **"My body releases the day with ease."**
- **"Cortisol lowers naturally; melatonin rises fully."**
- **"I enter rest, healing, and emotional softness."**
- **"My hormones reset in peace as the night begins."**
- **"I am safe to rest. I am safe to restore."**

ANYTIME EMERGENCY RESET AFFIRMATIONS

Use these when overwhelmed, stressed, unbalanced, or dysregulated.

- **"I return to my center."**
- **"My hormones respond to calm, not chaos."**
- **"I soften. I breathe. I realign."**
- **"I am not lost—my compass is still with me."**

SECTION 3 — THE CANDLE + BREATH COMPASS RESET RITUAL

A symbolic hormonal reset you can perform in 3–10 minutes

Fire is one of humanity's oldest environmental signals. It communicates warmth, safety, nightfall, stillness, and transition. When paired with breath, it becomes a powerful endocrine-calming tool capable of resetting nighttime rhythms, dissolving cortisol spikes, and deepening melatonin flow.

You may use a single candle. Any scent or color is fine, but white, gold, or natural beeswax works beautifully.

THE FULL RITUAL

PHASE 1 — IGNITING THE COMPASS FLAME

1. Sit comfortably with a candle in front of you.
2. Dim lights or sit in a naturally darkened space.
3. Light the candle slowly, watching the flame steady itself.
4. Whisper: **"This flame is my center."**

Hormonal effect: decreases sympathetic activation; lowers cortisol spikes; signals your circadian system that a transition has begun.

PHASE 2 — FLAME BREATHING

1. Inhale gently through the nose for 4 seconds.
2. Exhale slowly through the mouth for 6–8 seconds, soft enough to flicker the flame but not extinguish it.
3. Repeat 7–10 cycles.
4. Watch the flame respond to your breath.
5. Let your breath and the flame fall into a shared rhythm.

Hormonal effect:

- The long exhale lowers cortisol.
- Slow breath stabilizes heart rate variability.
- The visual rhythm activates parasympathetic dominance.

PHASE 3 — COMPASS ALIGNMENT GAZE

1. Keep eyes softly focused on the flame.
2. Visualize the flame extending into four directions—north, south, east, west.
3. See each direction representing an endocrine cycle:
   - East — Cortisol
   - South — Testosterone
   - West — Melatonin
   - North — Estrogen
4. Watch the flame "pull" these directions into harmony.
5. Whisper: **"All directions align."**

Hormonal effect: creates coherent imagery that activates neural pathways controlling hormonal rhythm.

PHASE 4 — RELEASE INTO QUIET

1. Close your eyes slowly.
2. Feel the warmth of the candle in your chest.
3. Imagine the flame shrinking inward until it rests behind the sternum.
4. Take one more slow exhale.
5. Whisper: **"Compass reset."**

Hormonal effect: shifts the nervous system fully into parasympathetic mode, promoting deep hormonal recalibration.

PHASE 5 — EXTINGUISHING WITH INTENTION

1. Blow out the candle with a soft, controlled breath.
2. Watch the smoke curl upward—symbolizing release.
3. Say: **"My hormones follow the new rhythm."**
4. Sit for a moment in silence.

Hormonal effect: the final exhale triggers melatonin rise or cortisol reduction depending on timing (sunset vs sunrise use).

CLOSING NOTE FOR APPENDIX A

These tools are not merely symbolic—they are **biochemical interventions disguised as ritual**.

They use breath to lower cortisol.

Imagery to recalibrate hormonal rhythms.

Firelight to signal melatonin.

Affirmations to shift dopamine, serotonin, and emotional alignment.

Use them daily, and your endocrine system will begin to respond with consistency and clarity.

Your compass will remain oriented—no matter what storms arise.

Message from the Author:

I hope you enjoyed this book, I love astrology and knew there was not a book such as this out on the shelf. I love metaphysical items as well. Please check out my other books:

-Life of Government Benefits

-My life of Hell

-My life with Hydrocephalus

-Red Sky

-World Domination:Woman's rule

-World Domination:Woman's Rule 2: The War

-Life and Banishment of Apophis: book 1

-The Kidney Friendly Diet

-The Ultimate Hemp Cookbook

-Creating a Dispensary(legally)

-Cleanliness throughout life: the importance of showering from childhood to adulthood.

-Strong Roots: The Risks of Overcoddling children

-Hemp Horoscopes: Cosmic Insights and Earthly Healing

- Celestial Hemp Navigating the Zodiac: Through the Green Cosmos

-Astrological Hemp: Aligning The Stars with Earth's Ancient Herb

-The Astrological Guide to Hemp: Stars, Signs, and Sacred Leaves

-Green Growth: Innovative Marketing Strategies for your Hemp Products and Dispensary

-Cosmic Cannabis

-Astrological Munchies

-Henry The Hemp

-Zodiacal Roots: The Astrological Soul Of Hemp

- **Green Constellations: Intersection of Hemp and Zodiac**

-Hemp in The Houses: An astrological Adventure Through The Cannabis Galaxy

-Galactic Ganja Guide

Heavenly Hemp
Zodiac Leaves
Doctor Who Astrology
Cannastrology
Stellar Satvias and Cosmic Indicas
Celestial Cannabis: A Zodiac Journey
AstroHerbology: The Sky and The Soil: Volume 1
AstroHerbology:Celestial Cannabis:Volume 2
Cosmic Cannabis Cultivation
The Starry Guide to Herbal Harmony: Volume 1
The Starry Guide to Herbal Harmony: Cannabis Universe: Volume 2
Yugioh Astrology: Astrological Guide to Deck, Duels and more
Nightmare Mansion: Echoes of The Abyss
Nightmare Mansion 2: Legacy of Shadows
Nightmare Mansion 3: Shadows of the Forgotten
Nightmare Mansion 4: Echoes of the Damned
The Life and Banishment of Apophis: Book 2
Nightmare Mansion: Halls of Despair
Healing with Herb: Cannabis and Hydrocephalus
Planetary Pot: Aligning with Astrological Herbs: Volume 1
Fast Track to Freedom: 30 Days to Financial Independence Using AI, Assets, and Agile Hustles
Cosmic Hemp Pathways
How to Become Financially Free in 30 Days: 10,000 Paths to Prosperity
Zodiacal Herbage: Astrological Insights: Volume 1
Nightmare Mansion: Whispers in the Walls
The Daleks Invade Atlantis
Henry the hemp and Hydrocephalus

10X The Kidney Friendly Diet
Cannabis Universe: Adult coloring book

Hemp Astrology: The Healing Power of the Stars

Zodiacal Herbage: Astrological Insights: Cannabis Universe: Volume 2

Planetary Pot: Aligning with Astrological Herbs: Cannabis Universes: Volume 2

Doctor Who: Convergence Protocol – The Replicator War

Nightmare Mansion: Curse of the Blood Moon

The Celestial Stoner: A Guide to the Zodiac

Cosmic Pleasures: Sex Toy Astrology for Every Sign

Hydrocephalus Astrology: Navigating the Stars and Healing Waters

Lapis and the Mischievous Chocolate Bar

Celestial Positions: Sexual Astrology for Every Sign

Apophis's Shadow Work Journal: **:** A Journey of Self-Discovery and Healing

Kinky Cosmos: Sexual Kink Astrology for Every Sign

Digital Cosmos: The Astrological Digimon Compendium

Stellar Seeds: The Cosmic Guide to Growing with Astrology

Apophis's Daily Gratitude Journal

Cat Astrology: Feline Mysteries of the Cosmos

The Cosmic Kama Sutra: An Astrological Guide to Sexual Positions

Unleash Your Potential: A Guided Journal Powered by AI Insights

Whispers of the Enchanted Grove

Cosmic Pleasures: An Astrological Guide to Sexual Kinks

369, 12 Manifestation Journal

Whisper of the nocturne journal(blank journal for writing or drawing)

The Boogey Book

Locked In Reflection: A Chastity Journey Through Locktober

Generating Wealth Quickly:How to Generate $100,000 in 24 Hours

Star Magic: Harness the Power of the Universe

The Flatulence Chronicles: A Fart Journal for Self-Discovery

The Doctor and The Death Moth

Seize the Day: A Personal Seizure Tracking Journal

The Ultimate Boogeyman Safari: A Journey into the Boogie World and Beyond

Whispers of Samhain: 1,000 Spells of Love, Luck, and Lunar Magic: Samhain Spell Book

Apophis's guides:Witch's Spellbook Crafting Guide for Halloween

Frost & Flame: The Enchanted Yule Grimoire of 1000 Winter Spells

The Ultimate Boogey Goo Guide & Spooky Activities for Halloween Fun

Harmony of the Scales: A Libra's Spellcraft for Balance and Beauty

The Enchanted Advent: 36 Days of Christmas Wonders

Nightmare Mansion: The Labyrinth of Screams

Harvest of Enchantment: 1,000 Spells of Gratitude, Love, and Fortune for Thanksgiving

The Boogey Chronicles: A Journal of Nightly Encounters and Shadowy Secrets

The 12 Days of Financial Freedom: A Step-by-Step Christmas Countdown to Transform Your Finances

Sigil of the Eternal Spiral Blank Journal

A Christmas Feast: Timeless Recipes for Every Meal

Holiday Stress-Free Solutions: A Survival Guide to Thriving During the Festive Season

Yu-Gi-Oh! Holiday Gifting Mastery: The Ultimate Guide for Fans and Newcomers Alike

Holiday Harmony: A Hydrocephalus Survival Guide for the Festive Season

Celestial Craft: The Witch's Almanac for 2025 – A Cosmic Guide to Manifestations, Moons, and Mystical Events

Doctor Who: The Toymaker's Winter Wonderland

Tulsa King Unveiled: A Thrilling Guide to Stallone's Mafia Masterpiece

Pendulum Craft: A Complete Guide to Crafting and Using Personalized Divination Tools

Nightmare Mansion: Santa's Eternal Eve

Starlight Noel: A Cosmic Journey through Christmas Mysteries

The Dark Architect: Unlocking the Blueprint of Existence

Surviving the Embrace: The Ultimate Guide to Encounters with The Hugging Molly

The Enchanted Codex: Secrets of the Craft for Witches, Wiccans, and Pagans

Harvest of Gratitude: A Complete Thanksgiving Guide

Yuletide Essentials: A Complete Guide to an Authentic and Magical Christmas

Celestial Smokes: A Cosmic Guide to Cigars and Astrology

Living in Balance: A Comprehensive Survival Guide to Thriving with Diabetes Insipidus

Cosmic Symbiosis: The Venom Zodiac Chronicles

The Cursed Paw of Ambition

Cosmic Symbiosis: The Astrological Venom Journal

Celestial Wonders Unfold: A Stargazer's Guide to the Cosmos (2024-2029)

The Ultimate Black Friday Prepper's Guide: Mastering Shopping Strategies and Savings

Cosmic Sales: The Astrological Guide to Black Friday Shopping

Legends of the Corn Mother and Other Harvest Myths

Whispers of the Harvest: The Corn Mother's Journal

The Evergreen Spellbook

The Doctor Meets the Boogeyman

The White Witch of Rose Hall's SpellBook

The Gingerbread Golem's Shadow: A Study in Sweet Darkness

The Gingerbread Golem Codex: An Academic Exploration of Sweet Myths

The Gingerbread Golem Grimoire: Sweet Magicks and Spells for the Festive Witch

The Curse of the Gingerbread Golem

10-minute Christmas Crafts for kids

Christmas Crisis Solutions: The Ultimate Last-Minute Survival Guide

Gingerbread Golem Recipes: Holiday Treats with a Magical Twist

The Infinite Key: Unlocking Mystical Secrets of the Ages

Enchanted Yule: A Wiccan and Pagan Guide to a Magical and Memorable Season

Dinosaurs of Power: Unlocking Ancient Magick

Astro-Dinos: The Cosmic Guide to Prehistoric Wisdom

Gallifrey's Yule Logs: A Festive Doctor Who Cookbook

The Dino Grimoire: Secrets of Prehistoric Magick

The Gift They Never Knew They Needed

The Gingerbread Golem's Culinary Alchemy: Enchanting Recipes for a Sweetly Dark Feast

A Time Lord Christmas: Holiday Adventures with the Doctor

Krampusproofing Your Home: Defensive Strategies for Yule

Silent Frights: A Collection of Christmas Creepypastas to Chill Your Bones

Santa Raptor's Jolly Carnage: A Dino-Claus Christmas Tale

Prehistoric Palettes: A Dino Wicca Coloring Journey

The Christmas Wishkeeper Chronicles

The Starlight Sleigh: A Holiday Journey

Elf Secrets: The True Magic of the North Pole

Candy Cane Conjurations

Cooking with Kids: Recipes Under 20 Minutes

Doctor Who: The TARDIS Confiscation

The Anxiety First Aid Kit: Quick Tools to Calm Your Mind

Frosty Whispers: A Winter's Tale

The Infinite Key: Unlocking the Secrets to Prosperity, Resilience, and Purpose

The Grasping Void: Why You'll Regret This Purchase

Astrology for Busy Bees: Star Signs Simplified

The Instant Focus Formula: Cut Through the Noise

The Secret Language of Colors: Unlocking the Emotional Codes

Sacred Fossil Chronicles: Blank Journal

The Christmas Cottage Miracle

Feeding Frenzy: Graboid-Inspired Recipes

Manifest in Minutes: The Quick Law of Attraction Guide

The Symbiote Chronicles: Doctor Who's Venomous Journey

Think Tiny, Grow Big: The Minimalist Mindset

The Energy Key: Unlocking Limitless Motivation

New Year, New Magic: Manifesting Your Best Year Yet

Unstoppable You: Mastering Confidence in Minutes

Infinite Energy: The Secret to Never Feeling Drained

Lightning Focus: Mastering the Art of Productivity in a Distracted World

Saturnalia Manifestation Magick: A Guide to Unlocking Abundance During the Solstice

Graboids and Garland: The Ultimate Tremors-Themed Christmas Guide

12 Nights of Holiday Magic

The Power of Pause: 60-Second Mindfulness Practices

The Quick Reset: How to Reclaim Your Life After Burnout

The Shadow Eater: A Tale of Despair and Survival

The Micro-Mastery Method: Transform Your Skills in Just Minutes a Day

Reclaiming Time: How to Live More by Doing Less

Chronovore: The Eternal Nexus

The Mind Reset: Unlocking Your Inner Peace in a Chaotic World
Confidence Code: Building Unshakable Self-Belief
Baby the Vampire Terrier
Baby the Vampire Terrier's Christmas Adventure
Celestial Streams: The Content Creator's Astrology Manual
The Wealth Whisperer: Unlocking Abundance with Everyday Actions
The Energy Equation: Maximize Your Output Without Burning Out
The Happiness Algorithm: Science-Backed Steps to Joyful Living
Stress-Free Success: Achieving Goals Without Anxiety
Mindful Wealth: The New Blueprint for Financial Freedom
The Festive Flavors of New Year: A Culinary Celebration
The Master's Gambit: Keys of Eternal Power
Shadowed Secrets: Groundhog Day Mysteries
Beneath the Burrow: Lessons from the Groundhog
Spring's Whispers: The Groundhog's Prediction
The Limitless Mindset: Unlock Your Untapped Potential
The Focus Funnel: How to Cut Through Chaos and Get Results
Bold Moves: Building Courage to Live on Your Terms
The Daily Shift: Simple Practices for Lasting Transformation
The Quarter-Life Reset: Thriving in Your 20s and 30s
The Art of Shadowplay: Building Your Own Personal Myth
The Eternal Loop: Finding Purpose in Repetition
Burrowing Wisdom: Life Lessons from the Groundhog
Shadow Work: A Groundhog Day Perspective
Love in Bloom: 5-Minute Romantic Gestures
The Shadowspell Codex: Secrets of Forbidden Magick
The Burnout Cure: Finding Balance in a Busy World
The Groundhog Prophecy: Unlocking Seasonal Secrets
Nog Tales: The Spirited History of Eggnog
Six More Weeks: Embracing Seasonal Transitions
The Lumivian Chronicles: Fragments of the Fifth Dimension

Money on Your Mind: A Beginner's Guide to Wealth
The Focus Fix: Breaking Through Distraction
January's Spirit Keepers: Mystical Protectors of the Cold
Creativity Unchained: Unlocking Your Wildest Ideas in 2025
Manifestation Mastery: 365 Days to Rewrite Your Reality
The Groundhog's Mirror: Reflecting on Change
The Weeping Angels' Christmas Curse
Burrowed in Time: A Groundhog Day Journey
Heartbeats: Poems to Share with Your Valentine
Dino Wicca: The Sacred Grimoire of Prehistoric Magick
Courage of the Pride: Finding Your Inner Roar
The Lion's Leap: Bold Moves for Big Results
Healthy Hustle: Achieving Without Overworking
Practical Manifesting: Turning Dreams into Reality in 2025
Jurassic Pharaohs: Unlocking the Magick of Ancient Egypt and Dino Wicca
The Happiness Equation: Small Changes for Big Joy
The Confidence Compass: Finding Your Inner Strength
Whispers in the Hollow: Tales of the Forgotten Beasts
Echoes from the Hollow: The Return of Forgotten Beasts
The Hollow Ascendant: The Rise of the Forgotten Beasts
The Relationship Reset: Building Better Connections
Mastering the Morning: How to Win the Day Before 8 AM
The Shadow's Dance: Groundhog Day Symbolism
Cupid's Kitchen: Quick Valentine's Day Recipes
Valentine's Day on a Budget: Love Without Breaking the Bank
Astrocraft: Aligning the Stars in the World of Minecraft
Forecasting Life: Groundhog Day Reflections

Bleeding Hearts: Twisted Tales of Valentine's Terror

Herbal Smoke Revolution: The Ultimate Guide to Nature's Cigarette Alternative

Winter's Wrath: The Complete Survival Blueprint for Extreme Freezes.

The Groundhog's Shadow: A Tale of Seasons
Burrowed Insights: Wisdom from the Groundhog
Sensual Strings: The Art of Erotic Bondage
Whispered Flames: Unlocking the Power of Fire Play
Forgotten Shadows: A Guide to Cryptids Lost to Time
Six Weeks of Secrets: Groundhog Day's Hidden Messages
Shadows and Cycles: Groundhog Day Reflections
The Art of Love Letters: Crafting the Perfect Message
Romantic Getaways at Home: Turning Your Space into Paradise
Purrfect Brews: A Cat Lover's Guide to Coffee and Companionship
The Groundhog's Wisdom: Timeless Lessons for Modern Life
The Shadow Oracle: Groundhog Day as a Predictor
Emerging from the Burrow: A Journey of Renewal
The Language of Love: Learning Your Partner's Love Style
Authorpreneur: The Ultimate Blueprint for Writing, Publishing, and Thriving as an Author
Weathering the Seasons: Groundhog Day Perspectives
Valentine's Day Magic: A Guide to Romantic Rituals
The Shadow Chronicles: Stories of Groundhog Day
Love and Laughter: Fun Games for Valentine's Day
AstroRealty: Unlocking the Stars for Property Success
The Groundhog's Path: A Guide to Seasonal Balance
Groundhog Day Diaries: Reflections in the Shadow
The Groundhog's Light: Illuminating the Path Ahead
Valentine's Traditions from Around the World
AI Wealth Revolution: Unlocking the Trillionaire Mindset
Love Rekindled: Reigniting Passion in Relationships
Single and Thriving: Self-Love on Valentine's Day
Emerald Legends: Mystical Tales of Ireland
Green Alchemy: Harnessing Nature's Magic
The Hearts of Horror: A Valentine's Day Nightmare

The Leprechaun's Guide to Wealth and Wisdom

Dancing with the Sidhe: Celebrating the Otherworld

Shamrocks and Shadows: Mysteries of the Green Isle

Emerald Energy: Harnessing Luck and Growth

The Gingerbread Golem's Valentine: A Sweetheart's Guide to Love and Enchantment

The Celtic Knot: Weaving Life and Destiny

Green Fire: Elemental Magic for St. Patrick's Day

Clover Chronicles: Finding Your Inner Luck

Ireland's Mystical Creatures: A Field Guide

Gingerbread Golem's Love Almanac

Prowl and Thrive: The Lion's Guide to Success

Love Alchemy: Transforming Your Life Through Heart Energy

WORLD DOMINATION: Woman's Rule 3:The New Life

The Midnight Rose: A Guide to Lunar Love Spells

The Forbidden Letters: Writing Your Own Love Prophecy

Luck and Lore: St. Patrick's Day for Modern Mystics

The Green Path: A Pagan Celebration of Renewal

The Dark Architect's Guide to Reprogramming Reality

Prankster's Paradise: A Guide to Harmless Hijinks

Manifest Your Reality: The Law of Attraction Simplified

The TARDIS Owner's Manual: Understanding the Doctor's Ship: *A complete guide to the TARDIS, its technology, secrets, and mysteries*

Starlit Romance: Astrology Secrets for Finding True Love

The Time Lord's Atlas: A Complete Guide to the Whoniverse: ***A breakdown of the locations, planets, and dimensions explored in Doctor Who***

Sweetheart Shadows: The Dark Side of Love and Attraction

February Fire: Reigniting Passion in Every Area of Life

The Self-Love Toolkit: 5 Ways to Embrace Who You Are

February Sparks: Ignite Your Dreams in 28 Days

March to Success: A 31-Day Action Blueprint
Ancient Paths: The 13 Sacred Principles of Dino Wicca
Echoes of Tomorrow: Navigating the AI Revolution
The Wellness Blueprint: Balancing Mind, Body, and Soul
Green Horizons: Sustainable Living for a Better Tomorrow
The AI Wealth Code: How to Make Millions with Automation
AI-Powered Creativity: Writing, Art, and Music for Profit
Extinction Rites: Rebirthing Your Soul Through Prehistoric Magick
Sacred Serpents tarot
Celestial Enchantment blank journal
Star Strains
Culinary Journeys: Exploring Global Flavors at Home
The Hollowvale Curse
The Hollowvale Harvest
The Egg of Transformation: Awakening Your Inner Power
Blooming Into Power: A Wiccan Guide to Spring Awakening
The Nightmare Nexus: The Third Doctor's Perilous Haunting
Digital Detox: Reclaiming Your Life in a Connected World
Ostara's Path: Walking the Spiral of Renewal
The Sacred Hare
Financial Freedom: Building Wealth in the Modern Age
Spring's Cauldron: Stirring the Waters of Change
The Hollowvale Pact
Quantum Consciousness: The Science of Reality Shifting
The Hollowvale Hunger
The Sacred Waters Within: A Witch's Guide to Hydrocephalus Magick
The Raven's Nest: Building a Life of Unshakable Stability
AI and the Human Mind: The Future of Intelligence
The Hollowvale Reckoning
Timeless Love: Building and Maintaining Lasting Relationships

The Raven's Roar: Unlocking Unstoppable Confidence
Raven Sight: Awakening Intuition and Inner Wisdom
The Butterfly Effect: Small Changes, Big Transformations
Taming the Boogeyman: How to Conquer Your Inner Fears
The Magick of Green: Awakening Earth's Energy in You
The Entrepreneurial Mindset: Secrets to Business Success
The Hollowvale End
The Shadow Luck Ritual: Reclaiming Power from Your Dark Side
Spring Magick for Beginners: A Simple Guide to Seasonal Energy Work
Doctor Who: The Hollowvale Conundrum
The March of Miracles: Unlocking Synchronicities in Spring
Unveiling the Cosmos: A Guide to Stargazing and Space Exploration
The Ultimate Guide to Surviving an Economic Collapse
The AI Gold Rush: How to Profit from the AI Revolution
Bastet's Shadow: The Hidden Power of Feline Magick
The Bastet Codex: Unlocking the Goddess's Magickal Secrets
Purring Spells: Harnessing Bastet's Healing Frequencies
Bastet's Nine Lives: Rebirth, Transformation, and Immortality Spells
Primal Currents: Hydrocephalus Magick in the Path of Dino Wicca
The Digital Gold Rush: Mastering E-Commerce and Online Sales
Future Shock: Adapting to the Next Decade of Change
The Quantum Mindset: Think Like a Billionaire
Sacred Motherhood: Awakening the Divine Feminine Within
The Mother's Spellbook: Enchantments for Love, Protection, and Prosperity
The Witch's Guide to Parenting: Raising Empowered and Intuitive Children

The Magick of Motherhood: Reclaiming Your Power Through Rituals

The Pagan Path to Self-Love: A Goddess's Guide to Worth and Confidence

Wild Woman Magick: Unleashing Your Primal Power

The Money Magnet Blueprint: Unlocking Unlimited Wealth

Biohacking 101: Unlock Your Body's Full Potential

The Wild Father: A Pagan Guide to Strength and Wisdom

The Sacred Masculine: Unlocking Your Inner Power

The Druid's Compass

The Warrior's Mindset

The Father's Fire

Odin's Path

Ancestral Bonds

The House That Whispers

The Magician's Code

The Wild Hunt

The Green Man's Path

The Altar of Success

The Shadow and the Sword

The High Priestess's Guide to Energy Healing

The Lunar Mother

The Sacred Self-Care Grimoire

The Womb Wisdom Codex

The Wheel of the Mother

The Witch's Guide to Manifestation

The Q2 Reset

The Ultimate Guide to AI-Powered Passive Income

Escape the 9-5

AI Feline Fortunes

The Tear-Stained Grimoire

Razorblade Runes

Cemetery Sirens

The Midnight Wristwatch
The Town That Forgets
AI Horror & Creepypasta
The Hollow Frequency
The Breach Echo
The Quiet Between Worlds
The Sigil of Tharan-Khul
Summon the Vault of Y'ha'ten
The Becoming Codex
The Profit of Az'ra-nar
The Drowned Logos
Echoes of the Eldritch Will
The Deep Ledger
Necronomicon of Networth
Covenant of the Wealthwyrm
The Whisperer's Manifesto
The Rites of Azh-K'luth
The Ark of the Crawling Coin
The Tithe of Shadows
Inkheart Abyss
The Timewinds of Y'ha-nthlei
The Spiral Labyrinth of Azag-Nirrh
The Gallifreyan Heresy of the Black Pharaoh
The Psalms of Nyog-Sotha
Black Rain Alchemy
The Infinite Maw
The Entropic Blueprint
The Oracle of Sh'guul
The Book of Breach
The Drowned Saint's Testament
Dreamcraft of the Sleeper God
The Silence Market
Cthonomics: The Dark Wealth Algorithm

Invocation of the Ten-Eyed King
Wealthbound to the Wyrm Below
Become the Unnameable
Codex of the Sovereign Flame
Rituals of Relentless Becoming
The Shadow Ascends
The Eyes Beneath You
The Will That Wakes Worlds
Silence Is a Weapon
The Mirror That Screams
The Whisper Between Moments
The Mind That Devours Fear
The Myth of the Finished Self
The Architect of Your Madness
The Voice You've Buried
The Discipline of Madness
Stormborn: Awakening Your Inner Tempest
The Mind That Ate Time
Unbind Your Becoming
The Pact You Owe Yourself
The Devourer's Diet
The Acid That Carves the Path
The Tower You Must Burn
The Breath Between Worlds
Speak Like the Deep
The Labyrinth Within
The Spine of the Sea God
Rejection Is a Portal
The Crown You Refused
The Scar Is the Spell
The Lightless Flame
The Habit of Becoming Horrific
ChickenJockey Chaos

The Gatekeeper Within
You Are Not Your Name
The Compass of the Mad
The Archive of Unsent Letters
What the Mirror Can't Show You
The Knife You Needed
Worship Nothing, Become Everything
The Other Voice
The Body the World Forgot
The Vein of the Void
The Black Bone Codex
The Puzzle of the Hidden Self (Millennium Puzzle)
The Eye That Sees the Lie *(Millennium Eye)*
The Ring of Return (Millennium Ring)
The Rod of Relentless Will *(Millennium Rod)*
The Tally of the Soul (Millennium Tauk/Necklace)
The Key to the Locked Timeline (Millennium Key)
The Scale of Sacred Decisions (Millennium Scales)
Inferno Bites: The UnOfficial Minecraft Lava Cookbook
Rot in the Attic
Prana: The Hidden Force of Your Infinite Self
The Shadow Realm Within: Transforming Darkness Into Destiny
The Borderland Collapse
Claws of Protection: Bastet's Defensive Magick
Mr. Ring-a-Ding's Madness
Yugioh Astrology: Celestial Deckcraft and Duel Destiny (2026–2027 Edition)
The Seal You Signed: Unlocking the Power You Once Feared
The Puzzle of Infinite Minds: Unlocking the Mentalism Hidden Within
The Eye That Mirrors the All: Secrets of Inner Reflection
Doctor Who: The Toymaker's Broadcast

The Rod of Eternal Flow: Commanding the Currents of Vibration

Golden Eyes of Bastet: Enhancing Psychic Vision

The Key of Dual Forces: Balance Within the Polarity

The Scales of Living Rhythm: Timing the Dance of Life

The Necklace of Hidden Cause: Weaving the Webs of Fate

The Ring of Secret Masters: Rising Through the All Within All

Daggers of the Dying Deep

Bastet's Wealth and Fortune Magick: Prosperity Rituals of the Goddess

The Tide that Speaks

The Scrolls of Petosiris: 13 Rituals from the Feathered Eye

Petosiris and the Living Plague of Osirion

Feline Fire: Bastet's Passion and Love Magick

The Star Altar of Petosiris

Bastet's Whiskers: Supernatural Sensory Magick

The Bastet Grimoire

Feeding the Shadows

The Mouthless Prayer

The Spiral Wound

Becoming the Ibis: Lessons from Petosiris's Mind

The Crimson Coven: Cola Magick for Sweet Dominion

Sacred Cat's Paw

The Soda Zodiac: A Flavor for Every Sign

Covenant of the Crawling Flame

The Ink of Ish'Zur

Frothroot: The Thirst That Ate the World

The Golden Glyphs of Prosperity

The Etherbind Codex

Echoes of the Resistance: Reclaiming the You That Survived

Harnessed Minds: Breaking Free from Mental Control

The Eyes in the Smoke

Rootwake: The Carbon Covenant
Skitter Logic: Unlearning the Fear That Built You
Doctor Who: The World That Froths
Rootwake: The Fizz That Rewrites Flesh
Rootwake: Frothfather of the World
The Holly Pact: Blood Beneath the Mistletoe
The 2nd Mass Principle: Building Unbreakable Tribes
Web of Wits: A Survival Guide to Encounters with Anasi the Spider (Aunt Nancy)
The Hexbreaking Handbook: Effective Spells to Remove Curses
Pop Alchemy: Transform Your Life One Sip at a Time
The Mason Code: Leading in Unleadable Times
Petosiris and the Fifth Chamber of Thoth
The Ether Seed Within
The Parent of Tomorrow
Petosiris's Pyramid of Perpetual Wealth
Unlearn the World
Grimoire of the Hollow Tongue
Zodiac Weeds: Finding Your Strain Through the Stars
Aquarius Rises in the Bank
The Sugar God's Smile
The Skinclock Reversal: Biohacking the Face of Time
Debtburn: How to Obliterate What You Owe Forever
The Ice Cream Oracle: What Your Cone Says About Your Future
Silence Is Sovereignty: The Power of Being Unreadable
The Wind That Whispers Through Stone
Path of the Four Directions
Doctor Who: The Maestro's Symphony of Endings
Oxygen Grail: Breathing to Undo the Clock
Zodiacal Collapse: When Stars Devour Time
Teachings from the Red Sand Silence

Doctor Who: Omega – The Broken Equation
Memory Wipe Your Past: Start Over Like a MiB
Mitochondria Prime: Ignite the Core of Youth
A Nest of Roaches
Grub from the Galaxy: MiB Recipes You'll Never Forget
Whiskers of Power: Bastet's Guide to Inner Sovereignty
The Gift Must Cost Them: Negotiation Through Unequal Exchange
The Worm Guys' Wealth Code: Hustle Like an Alien
Bug Out: The Edgar Method for Ruthless Goal Setting
Weaving Life with Spiderwoman's Pattern
Doctor Who: The Rani's Renaissance
How to Get a Job (If You're a Puppygirl)
Speak Through Others: The Art of Proxy Power
T-Rex Your Trauma: Reclaim the Power of Your Primal Self
The Black Briefcase: How MiB Stay Wealthy in Silence
The Thirst Beyond Reason: Understanding Diabetes Insipidus From the Inside Out
Backwoods Witchcraft for Billionaires: The Pagan Path from Dirt Roads to Gold Roads
The Moonshine Grimoire: Fermented Spells for Abundance
The Nameless Geometry
The Wraith's Mixtape: Spellcasting with Songs of Sorrow
The Gallifreyan Gentleman: Silent Wealth, Sonic Confidence, and the Doctor's Code of Living
Sugar Water Confidence
Dino Totems: Spirit Guides from Earth's First Gods
Pumpkin Sigils & Ritual Smoke
The Hózhó Compass
The Distortus Discipline – Order from Inner Mutation
Witchcraft for the Cold-Blooded Soul
Moonlight Over the Blessingway
Water, Interrupted: When the Body Forgets How to Hold On

Deformed but Divine: Embracing Your Asymmetry
Hexes in the Henhouse: The Farm Witch's Guide to Power
The Reversed Flame: A Grimoire of Inverted Power
Salt, Cells, and Sanity: Reclaiming Balance with Diabetes Insipidus
King of the Broken: Crowning the Flawed Self
Moonlight Scars: Emo Moon Magick and the Art of Lunar Sorrow
Noose Spells: Magick of the Hanging Rope
The Goth Cathedral: Rituals of the Broken and Beautiful
The Cretaceous Codex: Dino Spirits and Fossil Magick
The Turkey Bones Ritual
Nine Lives of Manifestation: Unlocking Bastet's Reality Codes
Chaos Muscles: Building Strength from Twisted Pain
Emo Blood Magick: The Veins of Power
The 3AM Flood: Nighttime Urination, Sleep Loss, and the DI Spiral
The Silence Between the Stars
The Lemon Method: Sour Your Way to Success
Starlit Sovereign
The Rite of Twelve Gates: Walking the Gates of the Duat.
Cornbread and Conjure: Recipes for Riches and Rootwork
The Black Rose Rituals: Emo Love Spells and Obsession Magick
The Eternal Goodbye: Death Magick and Rebirth Rituals
Sinkrot: The Drain That Remembers
The Hybrid Mindset: Thinking Beyond Evolution
Bone Dry: Navigating Dehydration Before It Breaks You
Wreathcraft: Winter Sigils and Yuletide Spells
The Rite of Twelve Mouths
S'mores of the Damned: Haunted Recipes for Halloween Night

Rethink the Drink: A Beverage Survival Guide for DI Warriors

The Shadow Chord: Guitar Magick and Sonic

Malformed Yet Majestic: Leading When You Feel Wrong Inside

The Cursed Diary: Ink-Stained Spells of the Emo Soul

Anxiety Off Switch: Emergency Reset for a Fried Nervous System

The Energy Heist: How to Take Back Your Life from Drainers

Beyond the Bathroom: Rebuilding Your Social Life With DI

Coyote's Gift for Decision Makers

Ghoul-Goo: Spooky S'mores You'll Die For

Echoes in the Mirror: Scrying and Self-Destruction Magick

Thread and Thorn: Stitching Spells from Rural Cloth

The Mogwai Mind: Building Untouchable Wealth from Small Ideas

Be Your Own Guide: Trust Your Inner Compass

Hormones in Chaos: The Endocrine Puzzle of Diabetes Insipidus

ChronoCleanse: Detox Your Biological Timeline

The Limb You Hide Is the One That Saves You

Leaves, Bones, and Whisper Spells

The Dinosaur Mindset: Prehistoric Tactics for Modern Wealth

Clawing Back Control: A Bastet Method for Boundaries and Empowerment

Samhain Codes of the Forgotten

Orange Alchemy: The Autumnal Spellbook

Monster Within, Master Without

The Sigil That Sleeps

Hearthcraft: Yule Hearth Sigils and Winter Warmth Spells

Temple of the Purring Moon: Rituals from Bastet's Lineage

When the Earth Remembers Your Footsteps

Food for Mood: Eat to Heal Depression, Not Just Survive It
Witch of the Kudzu Vine: Southern Pagan Wealth Secrets
The Invisible Diagnosis: Advocating for Yourself With DI
The Coffin's Lullaby: Sleep Magick and Nightmares as Portals
Ashes of the Will: Rituals for Erasing the Self
The Fracture Rite: Shattering the Magickal Core
Funeral Candles: The Art of Emo Flame Magick
The Black Grimoire: A Blank Ritual for Writing in Absence
Phantom Thirst: A Halloween Survival Guide for Diabetes Insipidus
The Hollow Crown: Emo Royalty and Magick of the Outcast King
Sandpainting for the Soul
Falling Into Balance: Using the Extra Hour to Recalibrate Life
100 Southern Superstitions That Still Work
The DI Child: A Parent's Guide to Raising Hydrated, Happy Kids
The Jungle of Shame: Escaping the Hidden Lab of Doubt
The Witch's Toast: S'mores Spells and Creepy Confections
The Hoodoo Pantry: Spells from the Mason Jar
The Immortal Fortune: Secret Wealth Lessons from Captain Jack Harkness
The Specter's Embrace: Magick for Channeling Ghostly Lovers
Grateful Waters: A Thanksgiving Survival Guide for Diabetes Insipidus
The Seizure Gospel
Harvestbind: Autumn Sigils and Samhain Spells
Doctor Who: The Algorithmic Awakening
Silent Nights, Steady Waters: A Christmas Survival Guide for Diabetes Insipidus
The Extra Hour Effect: How One Hour Can Transform Everything

Blade Between the Breaths

Running with the Mountain Shadows

Echoes of the Failed Experiment – Becoming a Living Legacy

Swamp Witches & River Ghosts: Real Southern Hauntings

Cornbread Prophecies: Magical Recipes from a Southern Table

Doctor Who: The Signal in the Star

Bloomcraft: Spring Sigils and Equinox Enchantments

Vanisher: How to Disappear from the Internet Without Losing Your Life

The Ultimate Christmas Cookie Cookbook

The Unbreakable Parent: How to Mentally Survive Raising Kids in a Broken World

Time Debt: How to Reclaim the Hours You Didn't Know You Lost

One Month, One Million: Unconventional Cash Creation Tactics

Doctor Who: The Cyber Conversion Protocol

Black Friday Frenzy: The Art of Finding Hidden Online Deals

The Grimoire Buried Under the Apple Tree

Digital Couponing Masterclass: Your Step-by-Step Guide to Black Friday Savings

The Fire Inside the Flint

Shadows on the Ceiling: The Emo Guide to Astral Magick

The Bone-Eaters Beneath Us

Black Friday Bundle Blueprint: Creating Irresistible Product Packages for Maximum Sales

Thirteen Nights of Unbinding

Doctor Who: Engines of Influence

Pumpkin Spice Alchemy: Recipes of Fire and Frost

When Raptor Met Rexy: Prehistoric Lessons in Wild Romance

Oblivion's Candle: Burn the Path Behind You

Campfire Curses and Chocolate: A Halloween S'mores Grimoire
The Wallet That Wasn't Mine: Breaking Free from Inherited Scarcity
The Cola Zodiac: What Your Fizz Says About Your Fate
Frostfire Fortune: Unlocking Winter's Hidden Prosperity
Signal Jamming: Detox Your Brain from Info Overload
The Dust of the Forgotten Rite
The Golden Cat Sigils: Drawing Power in Bastet's Name
Mud Magick: The Prosperity of Getting Dirty
Savory Spicefall: Beyond the Pumpkin Pie
Pumpkin Spice Apothecary Kitchen
The Pumpkin Spice Economy: Turning Trends into Billions
The Ember Veil: 13 Nights of Fire Magick
Financial Freeze: When Earning Triggers Panic
The Gingerbread Alchemist: Sweet Recipes with a Twist
Biosynth Power: Programming Yourself from Scratch
Echoes from the Talking Circle
Truffle Alchemy: Fungus of Fortune
Spores of Power: The Truffle Witch's Handbook
Doctor Who: The Tower That Speaks
The Mycelium Veil: Truffle Magick Unbound
Broke But Ashamed: Healing the Shame Wound of Debt
The Evergreen Mind: Growth Through Winter Stillness
The Black Veil Truffle Rite
The Voice Beneath Symbols
Witchlight on the Bayou: Swamp Spells for Sovereignty
I Grew Up Poor and Now I Sabotage My Success
The Lantern of Hollow Souls
Shutdown Survival: A Citizen's Guide to Thriving When Government Stops
When Abundance Feels Like a Threat: Healing the Hidden Fears of Enough

The Scarecrow Grimoire
Owls of the October Veil
Candlewax and Curses: A Halloween Spellbook
Excavating the Inner Fossil – Transforming Fossilized Thoughtforms into Tools of Power
The Yule Witch's Spellbook: Magick for the Holiday Season
Haunted Christmas: Ghost Stories for Winter Nights
The Christmas Survival Guide: Thriving Through the Chaos
The Bone Orchard Rites
Haunted Commerce: The Ghost in the Marketplace
When Money Triggers the Inner Child
Silent Night with the Silence: A Christmas Thriller
The Lightning Crown: Living and Leading Through Seizures
TARDIS Tidings: Festive Stories from the Whoniverse
Autumn Reset: Slowing Down Without Falling Behind
The Trillion Dollar Soul: Rewriting the Currency of Reality
Truffle Eclipse Magick
Micro-Manifestations: Quick Magick That Works
5-Minute Rituals for Busy Witches
The Marshmallow Massacre: Halloween Treats with a Sinister Twist
Blood and Blackberry Thorns
Magickal Mornings: Rituals for a Blessed Christmas Day
Embers of the All-Hallows Fire
The Pumpkin Market Collapse
The Hour You Gained: Transforming Time Into Power
The Chamber Must Be Sealed: Mastering the Power of Controlled Access
The Cursed Manuscript of Petosiris
The Festive Hearth: Creating Holiday Traditions
Darkness Rising: Thriving as Nights Grow Longer
Harvesting Time: Turning the Year's End Into Your New Beginning

Petosiris and the 13th Zodiac Key
Wagewound: When Paychecks Become Identity Prisons
Walls That Watch
The Silent Feast: Rituals of Power in the Longest Night
The Distortus Legacy : Becoming a Deformed King in a Perfect World
The Hollow Masks
The Gratitude Furnace: Forging Gold from Thanks
Feast of Inner Gold: Eating for Energy and Enlightenment
Haunted Commerce: The Season of Spending Spirits
Fear Bonds: How Panic Creates Profit
Black Friday E-Commerce Playbook: Sales Tactics to Skyrocket Your Holiday Revenue
Budgeting for Black Friday: A Holiday Savings Planner
Haunting the Harvest Moon
The Warrior's Water: Emergency Preparedness for People With DI
The First Sip of the Year: A New Year's Survival Guide for Diabetes Insipidus
Doctor Who: The Thirteenth Node
The Unseen Struggle: Mental Health, Anxiety, and Chronic Thirst
The Hearth's Hidden Ledger: Counting Energies as Currency
The Gift Alchemist: Turning Any Offering Into Gold
The Papyrus of the Bound Spirit
The Magick of Leftovers: Transmutation in the Fridge
Frost and Fortune: Christmas Wealthcraft for the Modern Magus
Last-Minute Gifts: Creative Ideas on a Budget
10 Secrets to Surviving Holiday Crowds
The Witch's Dow Jones
The Witches' Graveyard Shift
Pumpkin Sigils: Carving Rites for Midnight Power

The Secret Shopper's Black Friday Guide: How to Get Early Access and VIP Deals

Fever in the Foundation

The Neuralyzer Reset: Reprogram Your Morning Routine

Lightning Lessons of the White Painted Woman

The Enchanted Snowflake

The Magic Sip: Surviving Disney Parks with Diabetes Insipidus

The One Who Draws Through You

Santa's Secrets: A Magical Holiday Planner

Silent Bells, Loud Miracles: Self-Help for the Season of Stillness

The Sugar Spell Codex: Confectionary Magick of Christmas

Autumn Hexcraft: Fallen Leaves, Fallen Barriers

Sleep Like a Fortress: Build a Life Where Insomnia Can't Survive

Nowhere Was Ever Home

Christmas Under the Stars: A Celestial Holiday Guide

Rentproof: How to Never Be Evicted Again

Workless: Escape the 9-5 Without Being Broke

The Gilded Gift: A Wealth Altar for Christmas Morning

The Black Friday Grimoire

The Hollowing: Ceremonies of Spiritual Collapse

Doctor Who: The Nameless Signal

Where the Eagle Hides His Courage

The Dwarf Tyrant's Ascent: Claiming Power in a World of Giants

The Currency of the Dead: Trading with Spectral Bankers

The Icebound Witch: Survival and Magick in the Cold

The Emergency Money Mind: Constant Crisis, Zero Calm

Thirst & Roses: A Valentine's Survival Guide for Diabetes Insipidus

Springing Into Clarity: Mastering the Energy Shift of Daylight Saving

Speed of the Nanotyrant: Agile Strategies for Life's Hunt

The 90-Day Reset: A Science-Backed Guide to Reinvent Yourself Before the New Year

The Coil of Thorns

Timegates Unleashed

Dopamine Fasting 2.0: Rewiring Your Brain in a World of Overstimulation

The Nanotyrannus Mutation: Embracing Your Differentiated Form

Unwritten January: How to Use the Blank Page of the Year to Re-Author Your Life

Feast of the Forgotten Spirits: Ancestor Magick for the Holidays

The Burnout Codex: A System for Thriving Beyond Stress

I Don't Deserve to Have Money

When the King Doesn't See You: The Shadow Predator's Guide

The Reset Ritual :A Guide to Shedding Last Year's Weight—Emotional and Physical—by Spring Cleaning Your Soul

Calendar Alchemy: Learn to Bend Time and Productivity around Your Natural Rhythms

The Mirror Contract: A One-Sentence Agreement with Yourself that Unlocks Real Change

The Nile Formula: Sacred Flow for Millionaire Minds

Forward Momentum: Productivity Rituals for the Lost Hour

Harvest Gold: Wealth Magick of Pumpkin Spice Commerce

The Magick of Christmas Lights: Illuminating Holiday Rituals

Cranberry Crown: Royal Self-Worth through Ritual Meals

Petosiris and the Worms of the Feathered Throne

The Evergreen Equation: Self-Help for Sustained Growth

The Rain Will Wash Us Away: Emo Weather Magick

Snowlight Shadows: Magick Under Frozen Stars

Doctor Who: Merger of Empires

The Light Within the Feast: Magickal Wealth of Yuletide Flame

Momentum Machines: Small Habits Designed to Snowball into Unstoppable Forward Motion

Calm Spells: Magickal Solutions for Anxiety Relief

Santa's Final List: The Naughty Never Leave

The Mystic's Guide to Banishing Worry

The Silence Dividend: Turning Quiet Mornings into Compounding Growth All Year

Charmed Stillness: Rituals to Ease the Mind

Blood Spiral Ascension

The Vanishing Heart Invocation

Crystal Calm: Harnessing Stones for Anxiety

The Nano Tyrant Code: Strength in the Small Predator

The Energy Ledger: Accounting Methods for Vitality, Not Just Money

Snowglobe Mindset: Shake Up Your Thoughts, Settle Into Peace

The Weight of the Feather: Anubis's Codes for Soul Balance

Pocket Peppermint Power: Tiny Rituals for Big Holiday Energy

Shadowkeeper of the Golden Jackal: Anubis's Path to Energetic Protection

The Witch's Breath: Anxiety Relief Through Magickal Breathing

The Tiny Ember: Pocket Motivation for Cold Days

Stocking Sorcery: Mini Spells for Holiday Luck and Prosperity

Warm Hands, Steady Heart: Micro Grounding for Winter Anxiety

The Jackal's Lantern: Guide-Lights for Walking the Dark Path

Anubis's Silent Steps: Rituals for Stealth, Peace & Emotional Quiet

The Bonewake Protocol

Extinction-Proof: How to Outlive Trends, Trauma, and Time

The Fourth Doctor: The Eccentric Wanderer

The Second Doctor: Chaos and Charm in the TARDIS (Patrick Troughton, 1966–1969)

The Third Doctor: Earthbound Defender of Time (Jon Pertwee, 1970–1974)

The First Doctor: Genesis of the Time Lord (William Hartnell, 1963–1966)

The Fourth Doctor: The Eccentric Wanderer *(Tom Baker, 1974–1981)*

The Fifth Doctor: Elegance and Empathy (Peter Davison, 1982–1984)

The Sixth Doctor: A Kaleidoscope of Conflict (Colin Baker, 1984–1986)

The Seventh Doctor: The Strategist of Shadows (Sylvester McCoy, 1987–1989)

The Eighth Doctor: A Time Lord's Renaissance (Paul McGann, 1996)

The War Doctor: A Time Lord's Burden (John Hurt, 2013)

The Ninth Doctor: The Healer of Worlds
(Christopher Eccleston, 2005)

The Tenth Doctor: The Lonely Hero (David Tennant, 2005–2010)

The Eleventh Doctor: The Madman in a Box (Matt Smith, 2010–2013)

The Twelfth Doctor: The Rebel with a Cause (Peter Capaldi, 2013–2017)

The Thirteenth Doctor: Breaking the Mold
(Jodie Whittaker, 2017–2022)

The Fourteenth Doctor: A New Beginning (David Tennant, 2022–2023)

The Fifteenth Doctor: Rewriting the Stars
(Ncuti Gatwa, 2023–2025)

Santa's Shortcut to Success: Micro Habits for a Better New Year

The Midnight Cocoa Manifesto: Comfort Rituals for Hard Nights

Why I Can't Save: Trauma Blocks to Financial Planning

Dino Brain, Mega Goals: Rewire Yourself for Savage Success.

Jurassic Profit: Unearth Your Inner Millionaire Fossil

Scales & Softness: Dating with Dino Heart

Carnotaurus Dreams.

Red Willow Thinking.

Reindeer Resilience: How to Keep Going When You're Exhausted

Candlewick Courage: Lighting Strength in Dark Seasons.

Elf-Mode Focus: Fast Attention Fixes for Busy Seasons

Futureproof Feelings: Emotional Skill-Building for Resilience No Matter What the New Year Brings

The 90-Day Rewire: Transform Your Neural Pathways Before Spring Blooms

Jolly Rich: Christmas Micro-Money Magick for Fast Prosperity.

Gingerbread Gratitude: Mini Practices for a Happier Holiday

Trauma-Spending: When Money Becomes a Drug

Goal Skeletons: Build Minimalist Frameworks for Resolutions That Last

The Snarl Strategy: Growling Back at a World That Silenced You

The Hourglass Reset: Reclaiming What the Clock Took

Yule Claw: Dino Rites of Light in the Darkness

Sacred Circles: Grounding Rituals for Anxious Souls

Clockstopper's Gut: Rebuilding the Core of Time

Winterfire Drive: Harness the Cold Season's Stillness to Ignite Deep Motivation

The 5-Minute Productivity Hack: Small Steps to Big Results

Light Ascending: A Self-Help Guide to Longer Days

Inner Economy: Trade Self-Doubt for Confidence Like a High-Value Currency

Simple Success: Decluttering Your Life for Better Results

The Resilient Mind: Thriving in Tough Times

The 2026 Playbook: Mastering the Year Ahead

The Spring Sleep Solution: Conquering Fatigue After Time Change.

Get Some Tarot cards: https://www.makeplayingcards.com/sell/apophis-occult-shop

Get some shirts: https://www.bonfire.com/store/apophis-shirt-emporium/

Instagrams:
@apophis_enterprises,
@apophisbookemporium,
@apophisscardshop
Twitter: @apophisenterpr1
Tiktok:@apophisenterprise
Youtube: @sg1fan23477
Hive: @sg1fan23477
CheeLee: @SG1fan23477

Podcast: Apophis Chat Zone: https://open.spotify.com/show/5zXbrCLEV2xzCp8ybrfHsk?si=fb4d4fdbdce44dec

Newsletter: https://apophiss-newsletter-27c897.beehiiv.com/

If you want to support me or see posts of other projects that I have come over to: **buymeacoffee.com/mpetchinskg**

I post there daily several times a day

Get your Dinowicca or Christmas themed digital products, especially Santa Raptor songs and other musics. Here: **https://sg1fan23477.gumroad.com**

Apophis Yuletide Digital has not only digital Christmas items, but it will have all things with Dinowicca as well as other Digital products.

www.ingramcontent.com/pod-product-compliance
Lightning Source LLC
LaVergne TN
LVHW022219200926
848481LV00006B/2029